LEARNING REASONABLE SALE PRICE STRATEGY

JOHN LOK

Copyright © John Lok
All Rights Reserved.

This book has been self-published with all reasonable efforts taken to make the material error-free by the author. No part of this book shall be used, reproduced in any manner whatsoever without written permission from the author, except in the case of brief quotations embodied in critical articles and reviews.

The Author of this book is solely responsible and liable for its content including but not limited to the views, representations, descriptions, statements, information, opinions and references ["Content"]. The Content of this book shall not constitute or be construed or deemed to reflect the opinion or expression of the Publisher or Editor. Neither the Publisher nor Editor endorse or approve the Content of this book or guarantee the reliability, accuracy or completeness of the Content published herein and do not make any representations or warranties of any kind, express or implied, including but not limited to the implied warranties of merchantability, fitness for a particular purpose. The Publisher and Editor shall not be liable whatsoever for any errors, omissions, whether such errors or omissions result from negligence, accident, or any other cause or claims for loss or damages of any kind, including without limitation, indirect or consequential loss or damage arising out of use, inability to use, or about the reliability, accuracy or sufficiency of the information contained in this book.

Made with ♥ on the Notion Press Platform
www.notionpress.com

Contents

Preface

Introduction

In our societies , any kinds of products or services must need to apply demand and supply economic theory to analyze whether the kind of product or service may be value to invent to sell or serve to their customers in consumer market, if the kind of product or service demand number is less, then it ought not to raise manufacturing number to avoid "low price " sale or if the kind of product demand number is more, then it ought raise manufacturing number to have enough number in order to raise " high price" sale to satisfy customers their needs to buy their products. However, whether your product or serive's demand number depends on supply number or your product or service's supply number depends on demand number in order to make ths sale price is reasonable high or low level and reasonable supply number valuation.
In my this book, I shall indicate some actual product or service social suitation to explain whether it is right time to these kinds of product or service of their sale price ought increase or demand in market demand and supply environment in order to avoid customers number reduce. Readers can learn sale price strategy of these sale cases studies.

Prologue

Contents

What is the difference between production orientation and societal marketing orientation and sales orientation to body shop ? p.191-200

Chapter 11 Reason of sales of ready meals in supermarket may help cooking food raise sale price

Case study change in the marketing environment on sales of ready meals to supermarket, such as Walt Mark strategy ? p.201-210

CHAPTER ONE

Explaining supply and demand economic theory

The difference between past and nowadays economists their demand and supply economic theory explanation?

The law of supply and demand defines the relationship between the price of a given good or product and the willingness of people to either buy or sell it. Generally, as the price of a good increases, people are willing to supply more and demand less. These economists had explained economic demand and supply theory as below:

Philosopher John Locke is credited with one of the earliest written descriptions of this economic principle in his 1691 publication, Some Considerations of the Consequences of the Lowering of Interest and the Raising of the Value of Money. Locke addressed the concept of supply and demand as part of a discussion about interest rates in 17th-century England. Many merchants wanted the government to lower the cap on interest rates charged by private lenders so that people could borrow more money and thus purchase more goods. Locke argued that the free-market economy should set rates because government regulation could have unintended consequences. If the lending industry were left alone, interest rates would regulate themselves, Locke wrote: "The price of any commodity rises or falls by the proportion of the number of buyers and sellers."

Sir James Steuart's Inquiry into the Principles of Political Economy, published in 1796, was the first known printed use of the term "supply and demand." When Steuart wrote his treatise on political economy, one of his main concerns was the impact of supply and demand on laborers.

Adam Smith dealt extensively with the topic in his 1776 epic economic work, The Wealth of Nations. Often referred to as the Father of Economics, Smith explained the concept of supply and demand as an "invisible hand" that naturally guides the economy. According to Smith, the invisible hand is the automatic pricing and distribution mechanisms in the economy. Smith described a society in which bakers and butchers provide products that individuals need and want, providing a supply that meets demand and developing an economy that benefits everyone. It is important to note that Smith's ideas haven't gone without critique over the years since his ideas were first published, though. Over time, his ideas have been added to in order to represent the changing times and include concepts such as marginal utility, comparative advantage, entrepreneurship, the time-preference theory of interest, and monetary theory.

One of Marshall's most important contributions to microeconomics was his introduction of the concept of price elasticity of demand, which examines how price changes affect demand. In theory, people buy less of a particular product if the price increases, but Marshall noted that in real life, this behavior was not always true. The prices of some goods can increase without reducing demand, which means their prices are inelastic. Inelastic goods tend to include items such as medication or food that consumers deem crucial to daily life. Marshall argued that supply and demand, costs of production, and price elasticity all work together.

Nowadays economists they explain demand and supply economic theory, they have some different to past economists whose explanation as below:

How Does Supply and Demand Work? The law of supply and demand is a theory that explains the interaction between the sellers of a resource and the buyers of that resource. Generally, as price increases, people are willing to supply more and demand less and vice versa when the price falls.

What does the bottom line mean. Despite the origins of the law of supply and demand beginning hundreds of years ago, it's still a topic frequently referenced and utilized today in economic theory and discussions. The theory has developed over time to accommodate recent technological and economical advancements, but the basic ideas of the theory remain largely the same.

Does demand depend on supply?

Supply and Demand Determine the Price of Goods and Quantities Produced and Consumed. Consumers may exhaust the available supply of a good by purchasing a given good or service at a high volume. This leads to an increase in demand. As demand increases, the available supply also decreases.

What does market demand depend on?

Market factors affecting demand of consumer goods. The demand for a good increases or decreases depending on several factors. This includes the product's price, perceived quality, advertising spend, consumer income, consumer confidence, and changes in taste and fashion.

Who controls the demand in supply and demand?

Supply and demand are in turn determined by technology and the conditions under which people operate. At one extreme, the market could be populated by a large number of virtually identical sellers and buyers (for example, the market for ballpoint pens).

What are the two laws of demand and supply?

The law of demand holds that the demand level for a product or a resource will decline as its price rises, and rise as the price drops. Conversely, the law of supply says higher prices boost supply of an economic good while lower ones tend to diminish it.

What factors affect demand and supply?

Price fluctuations are a strong factor affecting supply and demand. When a product gets expensive enough that the average consumer no longer feels it is worth it to buy the product, then the demand declines. This leads to cuts in production that will hopefully stabilize the product's value.

What factors affect demand and demand?

Demand may be defined as the quantity of a commodity that a consumer is able and willing to buy, at each possible price, over a given period of time. • Essential elements of demand are quantity, ability, willingness, prices, and period of time.

Which factors affect supply?

Generally, the supply of a product depends on its price and other variables such as the cost of production.

a. Price. Price can be understood as what the consumer is willing to pay to receive a good or service. ...

b. Cost of production. ...

c. Technology. ...

d. Governments' policies. ...

c. Transportation condition.

How does supply and demand work together?

It's a fundamental economic principle that when supply exceeds demand for a good or service, prices fall. When demand exceeds supply, prices tend to rise. There is an inverse relationship between the supply and prices of goods and services when demand is unchanged.

What happens to supply when demand increases?

An increase in demand, all other things unchanged, will cause the equilibrium price to rise; quantity supplied will increase. A decrease in demand will cause the equilibrium price to fall; quantity supplied will decrease.

What is the theory of demand?

Demand theory describes the way that changes in the quantity of a good or service demanded by consumers affects its price in the market, The theory states that the higher the price of a product is, all else equal, the less of it will be demanded, inferring a downward sloping demand curve.

What are the 4 basic laws of supply and demand?

1) If the supply increases and demand stays the same, the price will go down. 2) If the supply decreases and demand stays the same, the price will go up. 3) If the supply stays the same and demand increases, the price will go up. 4) If the supply stays the same and demand decreases, the price will go down.

The different types of demand are as follows:

i. Individual and Market Demand: ...

ii. Organization and Industry Demand: ...

iii. Autonomous and Derived Demand: ...

iv. Demand for Perishable and Durable Goods: ...

v. Short-term and Long-term Demand:

What creates demand for a product?

You can create demand for a unique product if you can manage to solve a persistent problem for the consumer. People are always running away from pain, and providing them with an outlet is a sure-fire way to create massive demand for your goods.

What are the 7 factors that affect supply?

The seven factors which affect the changes of supply are as follows: (i) Natural Conditions (ii) Technical Progress (iii) Change in Factor Prices (iv) Transport Improvements (v) Calamities (vi) Monopolies (vii) Fiscal Policy.

What can affect demand?

Factors Affecting Demand

Price of the Product. ...

The Consumer's Income. ...

The Price of Related Goods. ...

The Tastes and Preferences of Consumers. ...

The Consumer's Expectations. ...

The Number of Consumers in the Market.
What are the three factors affecting demand?
The demand for a product will be influenced by several factors:
Price. Usually viewed as the most important factor that affects demand.
...
Income levels. ...
Consumer tastes and preferences. ...
Competition. ...
Fashions.
What are the 4 factors of supply?
The four factors that can shift the supply curve include natural conditions, input prices, technology, and government.
What causes increase in supply?
If the cost of production is lower, the profits available at a given price will increase, and producers will produce more. With more produced at every price, the supply curve will shift to the right, meaning an increase in supply.
What causes supply changes?
A change in supply is an economic term that describes when the suppliers of a given good or service alter production or output. A change in supply can occur as a result of new technologies, such as more efficient or less expensive production processes, or a change in the number of competitors in the market.
Is supply and demand a good strategy?
When it comes to profit placement, supply and demand zones can be a great tool as well. Always place your profit target ahead of a zone so that you don't risk giving back all your profits when the open interest in that zone is filled.
How is demand created?
Demand creation is a process that fuels the revenue pipeline so the sales team can meet or exceed their quotas. In other words, it takes your big idea — the creative appeal of your brand — and turns it into sales. That sounds a lot like demand generation, which often gets confused with lead generation.
What are the two parts of demand?
Economists define demand as the quantity of a good or service that buyers are willing and able to buy at all possible prices during a certain time period. Notice that there are two components to demand: willingness to purchase and ability to pay.
Can we control demand?

If you're willing to think and act strategically, you can easily manipulate the laws of supply and demand. It should be surprising to learn, however, that by manipulating the laws of supply and demand, you can make more profit in less time and with far fewer headaches

How do you control demand?

Here are five short-term actions to improve your demand variability management plans in this time of uncertainty:

Maintain transparent, proactive relationships with your suppliers. ...

Activate alternate sources of supply. ...

Reduce lead times. ...

Update inventory policy and planning. ...

Align supply and demand management.

What are the 8 types of demand?

There are 8 states of demand: negative demand, no demand, latent demand, falling demand, irregular demand, full demand, overfull demand and unwholesome demand.

What is Demand?

Types of Determinants of Demand. Every factor has a unique impact on demand. ...

Price of the Product. ...

The Income of the Consumers. ...

Number of Buyers in the Market. ...

Consumer's Expectations. ...

Tastes and Preferences of The Consumers. ...

Complement Goods. ...

Substitute Product.

What is theory of supply?

The law of supply is a fundamental principle of economic theory which states that, keeping other factors constant, an increase in price results in an increase in quantity supplied. In other words, there is a direct relationship between price and quantity: quantities respond in the same direction as price changes.

What are the types of supply?

There are five types of supply—market supply, short-term supply, long-term supply, joint supply, and composite supply.

Which comes first supply or demand?

Demand comes first and it's followed by the corresponding supplies. Supply and demand are both very important to economic activity. Supply is the total amount of a particular good or service available at a given time to consumers at a given price. Demand is a representation of a consumer's desire to purchase goods and services; it acts as a measurement of a consumer's willingness to purchase a specific good or service at a given price. These two economic forces influence each other; they are both important for the economy because they impact the prices of consumer goods and services within an economy and the quantities produced and consumed. Supply and demand are both keys to understanding the economy because they reflect the prices and quantities of consumer goods and services within an economy.

What are the relationship between demand and supply?
According to market economy theory, the relationship between supply and demand balances out at a point in the future; this point is called the equilibrium price.
Economists and companies analyze the relationship between supply and demand when making strategic product decisions. Both economists and companies analyze the relationship between supply and demand when making strategic product decisions. The assumption behind a market economy is that supply and demand are the best determinants for an economy's growth and health.
Consumer Behavior Influences Demand
One way that companies or economists might analyze this relationship is to create graphs that chart the equilibrium price of certain goods and services in order to determine product development and their production schedule. Consumer behavior dictates which products are produced and sold because consumers create the demand that companies attempt to meet. As a result, companies may study consumer behavior in an attempt to understand the current demand and predict future demand. It is vital that companies maintain the capacity to produce enough of a good or service that they can satisfy consumer demands.
Supply and demand are two sides of the same market coin. Generally, supply is how much of something is available or will be produced at a certain price. Demand is how much of something people want to purchase or consume at a certain price. One way to develop a more precise relationship between the two is to consider how the price of something affects its supply and its demand. Generally when the price of a good goes up, so does the supply, since firms are willing to create more when they can

sell at higher prices. But when the price of a good goes up consumers will, at the same time, generally demand less. It is the interaction of supply and demand that determines how much will be produced and consumed and at what price, converging to a state known as equilibrium.

CHAPTER TWO

Human social job demand and supply relationship

The relationship between social change and human behavior

Human Behavioral network job brings social economic benefits

Whether human social job change it depends on social job demand more or job supply more? What does human network job mean ? Why may human network job be popular? Why human network job behavior may influence economy ?

Nowadays internet is popular to use. We can apply internet to find data , search any new things, even earn money. Why does internet may become huma network job source. For example, e-publish may be one kind of new human network job. Any authors may apply internet channel to help them to sell electronic or paper books from e-publisher web store. They may apply facebook, you tub etc. any online channel to promote themselves new books to let new readers to know whether when they may buy themselves favourable new topic books to read from electronic publisher web store.

Thus, future electronic publisher industry may help any authors to build internet network platform to help them to sell and promote ot advertise their any one new electronic or paper book topic to let global any one reader to choose to buy their any new topic books from electronic publisher web store easily and conveniently. However, it implies that electronic network platform author may be one kind of future new human network job in our societies.

How electronic network platform author job may bring economy benefit in macro economy view? A person can have few friends, contacts and still

be very influential if these few
friends and contacts are themselves highly influential, e.g. one author must not need to know any one reader in global society. When they like to choose any electronic books from electronic internet network platform. They may become the author's any one topic book buyer, when they feel the author's any one topic book is fun and attract they make decision to buth the strange author whose the topic book from electronic book publisher's platform web store conventiently in short time. Although, they are strangers, they do not know themselves , but the reader can understand what it way that made Google from writing platofrm to create new creative mind and typing network job method to replace traditional hand writing book method for global authors. It will be one kind of new human network writing job.

Hence, global any one reader can apply an innovative search engine , such as google.com to find whether whom author personal new topic books are value to read from internet.

Then, the electroniuc publisher's web store may be new book store platform sale network to help the author to sell many electronic or paper books from electronic network platform
in short time. So, internet may be future new network plaform to help global any one author to create network writing job absolutely. Furthermore, internet may be popular social media
to help any one author to build goold relationship between his/her readers. It is one kind of new network, human network job. New authors do not need to buy many paper books to prepare to put in any one book shop warehouse. Their every book can print on demand to reduce out of book stock in any one book shop. They may choose to sell either electronic books or paper books both from any one book publisher web store. So, electronic network platform may be one kind of good writing channel to help human authors to create income and it can also help authors to bring new creative mind and new topic fun content books to let readers to know and buy to read from electronic publisher network platform.

Why does human behavior may be one kind of new human network job to bring global economic advantages. ALthough, it may be free income or without inocme, but the person does the network behavior, his/her behavior may be bring advantages to influence many other people's health. For this case, when a worker in a coffee shop in an airport gets a vaccination aganinst the flu, it does not only helps him or her stay healthy, but also helps the many travellers who might otherwise have been inflected if that workers caught the flu. So, the externality , the result implies the vaccination of even a part of a community conveys benefits to the whole community. For example, governments pay special attention to the vaccinations of school children, teachers, health mothers, and the elderly, categories of people particularly susceptible not only to catching, but also to transmitting a disease.

It is not accidential that governments are heavily involved with vaccination . When there are externalities, free market, fail to persuade individual incentives with society's

their the worker's decision of whether to get a vaccine ends up attracting whether other people get sick. The workers might not fully take all these other people's potential suffering into account when making her or his vaccination decision.

As Stanford University does many suggestions, understand this and tries to help them make the right decisions and so providers free flu vaccines for its staff and students.

Small pockets of unvaccinated individuals can allow a disease to gain a spread more widely well-being. For example, parent weighing the costs and benefits of a vaccine for their child is not always thinking of the consequences of that vaccination to other people. THese are markets in which subsidizing or regulating behavior can make everyone better off. Because the reason for requiring that a child be vaccinated before enrolling in school is not just to protect that child, because each child's vaccination affects others via potential contagions.

On conclusion, it seems that many traditional paper book publish business begain to change to electronic book publish business. Due, to online technology existence, it influences many readers choose to buy electronic books to read. Hence, due to readers reading demand change which is from paper book reading habit to electonic book reading habit.Then,it explains that electornic book supply number depends on electronic book reader reading demand in economic view.

Robots take our jobs behavioral and economy influences

Robot job behavior brings economy influences

Whether robot labor needs are depended on employer labor demand more or robot labor number supply more? If one day robots can replace human to do simple, even complex jobs. They will bring what influences to our global societial economy.The popular economic refrain declares that the global middle class is dying and robots will soon take our jobs, e.g. shopping center customer service jobs, library service jobs, cinema ticket sale jobs, restaurant kitchen cooker jobs, even, bus drivers, taxi drivers etc. public transport driving jobs, accountant, doctors etc. professional jobs. Whether it is beautiful or petty matter if our future societies have many human jobs can be replaced to do from robots. Businessman must may reduce to employ employees and reduce to pay salary or wage, when robots can be replaced to do their employees tasks. But, societies must bring unemployement rate rises , due to societies will have many people loss jobs when their employers choose to buy robots to serve their clients or do any office tasks or customer service or cleaning etc. tasks.

In micro economy view, employers may save money in long term, but in macro economy view, it will cause unemployment ratio rises , even crime rate rises when there are many people lose jobs in societies. These models of doom, though, fail to account for the hundreds of businesses riding the waves of change in their industries when robots may be invented to replace human to do many simple , even complex tasks in our future societies.

WE may image that one small factory needs to manufacture fishes canes to sell to supermarket, the small , cheaper stuff and higher margin parts of the fishes manufacture industry. Before, this factory needs to employe many human factory workers need to help every fresh customer makeing the perfect fishing gear, designed for performance, durability, and cost in order to achieve to manufacture every fish cane in whole fished processing manufacturing stages. Every worker needs to spend about 15 to twenty minutes to finish every fish cane , till to delivery to any supermarket to sell. If this fish canes manufacturing factory can apply manufacturing robots to help them to finish any one working tasks , every robot can only spend five minutes to finish whole fresh fish cane manufacturing process. Thus, every robot can help this factory save 10 to 15 minutes time to finsh every fish cane manufacturing process. IN fact, time is money, because when every robot can help this factory to reduce 10 to 15 minutes time to compare human worker. Then, this factory can finish about 20 fish canes in one hour if it can use robot to help it to manufacture fish canes. Otherwise, if this

factory still use human workers to help it to manufacture fish canes, then it can finsh about 3 to 4 fish canes in one hour. SO, the manufacturing efficiency ensures that robots must help this fish manufacturing factory to raise fish canes number more than human workers. So, in robotic behavioral economy view, manufacturing robots must help this fish canes manufacturing factory to raise fish canes manufacturing number and deliver increasing number to supermarkets to prepare to sell every day. Robots can help this fish canes manufacturing factory bring manufacturing time saving, rising manufacturing efficiency, improving performance and reducing wages expenditure long time advantages in micro economy view. However, manufacturing robots can also bring disadvanages to society, e.g. increasing unemployment ratio, increasing crime rate,
this factory workers will lose jobs and income, they need earn social welfare from government and increasing government finance pressure in short time, even long time in macro economic view.

Stanford University graduate program in economics, Scott lecturer explained that "in demand and supply economic theory for robots supply and demand case, robots supply number increasing may influence human workers demand number decrease. It sometimes calls " the efficient frontier".
No specific human beings were mentioned in any of economics classes. As robots supply and demand in market case, They (robots) may be purely theoretical " agents" who reached to the most reasonable sale prices in order to persuade any one businessman buyer to make manufacturing robot buying decision whether robots can help him / her to bring how much saving time , saving money, saving cost, improving performance, efficiency economic benefit before he/she plans to reduce workers number when he/ she decides to apply robots to replace human workers in his/her factory or office or any service department, e.g. cinema ticket sale service, shopping center customer service, shopping center cleaning , supermarket customer service etc. service or sale tasks. When robots can replace human to do any one of these tasks in any organizations. So, robots may be human worker agents who reached to prices the way robots would react to a software command. There was nothing that explained why somc people thrived and others did n't or why truly brilliant, hardworking people could fail when much lazier folks succeeded." Having been admitted to the Stanford University graduate program in economics, Scott lecturer hoped to get his answers there.

How robots influence our future social changing? Using the right technology can be a boon to your business in this economy. For internet example, it is easier than ever to find well-matched customers all around the world, to stay in contact with them, and to more quickly design the products they want. If you focus solely on being cutting -edge, though you risk letting the technology

take over what should be very robust relationships with your customers , employees, and colleagues. IN nowaddays society, technoligical advances and cutomation, personal

relationships in business are more crucial than ever. I mean that robots can not replace human to serve clients to let them to feel more comfortable and passion more easily. For shoe shop case example, if the shoe shop apply one robot to serve its clients to replace human shoe salesperson to serve its shoe customers. Robots ensure that they can not persuade every shoe potential buyer to make shoe buying decision more easily when robots need to contact every shoe potential buyer. The reason is simple, because robots can not touch any one shoe buyer individual emotion very easier.

If the shoe buyer needs the robots to help him/her to choose any right shoe styles when he/she can not feel himself / herself can make the most right shoe style choice decision. The robots can not replace human shoe salesperson to make shoe style choice judgement more easily. They must need longer time to analyze whether which shoe style may be the most suitable to the shoe buyer. Otherwise, human shoe salesperson may attempt to make the most right shoe style choice decision to help any one shoe buyer to chooce the most right style shoe because he/she owns shoe style sale experience, shoe style knowledge, the most important reason is that they can feel every shoe customer individual emotion to touch whether he/she will feel comfortable or happy when they attempt to help every shoe customer to seek the most right shoe style in every shoe customer whole shoe searching processing. Othwerwise, serving robots are only one machine, they can not touch or feel every shoe customer individual emotion whether he/she feel comfortable or unhappy or happy when they need to contact them in whole shoe searching processing. Hence, I believe that some tasks robots can

not repalce human staff to do very easily. Otherwise, robots may bring disadvanatges to let any one businessman to loss his/her customers, due to robots can not touch every customer

emotion to compare human staff in service tasks more easily. Robots serving customer behaviors may cause money lose and customers number lose to the shop in micro economic view.

On conclusion, in demand and supply economic theory for robots supply and demand case, robots supply number increasing may influence human workers demand number decrease. So, it seems that robots number supply will be depended on global robots supply number more than robots demand number because when human began to accept robots to replace human to do general simple jobs in global labor market. Then, it means that global robots labor number must need to be increased in order to satisfy global businessmen workers number need. If any kinds of robot workers manufacture number is not enough to be supplied to let global future businessmen to buy, then robot supply will be shortage and they can not provide to satisfy global businessmen robots labour purchase need. So, future robot number will be depended on supply more than demand.

CHAPTER THREE

Human intellectual demand and supply behavior relationship

Intellectual human economic behaviors

What does intellectual human economic behaviors mean ? Human foolish behavior is depended on social enjoyment need more or material social supply more? I believe that when we choose or decide to do intellectual behaviors, then our societies will be influenced to bring economic growth in consequence.I shall attempt to indicate pollution case to explain how and why eithet our intellectual or foolish behaviors may bring economic growth or recession in consequence as below:

On one hand, for air pollution social case aspect example, if we only consider to buy cars to drive for working aim or holiday leisure aim. Then, our societies air will be polluted. Our health will be influenced to bad. Our car driving behaviors may cause global environment air pollution serously. In long tiem, global air pollution will bring our bodies health to be bad. Although, ourselves car driving behaviors may bring our driving travelling leisure enjoyment and comfortable feeling in short time, also we so not need to pay public transport fare often, but we need to compensate ourselves health economic intangible loss due to air pollution , when cars number increases, dirty air will cause ouselves health to become bad.

In the result, we will need to pay more medical expenditure when we are old age, due to ourselves bodies will become bad, due to we breathe global dirty air every day, due to ourselves cars pollute air in long time, e.g. 10 to 20 years, even 30 more without limited air pollution environment. So, driving cars behavior may be one kind of human foolish behavior and our foolish behavior may bring ourselves future long time medical expenditure absolutely.

One the other hand, water pollution social aspect, if we often keep much rubblish to pollute sea, oil exploration porcessing pollute ocean , ships gas pollute ocaen, then fishes will eat polluted food and drive dirty water, due to global ocean is polluted.

In fact, because human only to conside how to buy boats to carry on leisure enjoyment activities, or catch cruises to travel on the sea. Also, oil manufacturers only consider researching anywhere to find new oil exploration places to manufacture oil product, when their oil exploration processes pollute ocarn . Consequently, global fishes drink polluted warer or eat polluted food. They will have poison. SO, human will have high chance to eat poison polluted fishes, due to fishes are poison or are polluted. So, human is doing foolish activities, we only hope to find oil exploration places to pollute ocean or we only spend money to buy ticket to catch ships to travel anywhere in global ocean. All of these human foolish behaviors will bring pollution to global ocean. On consequently, we will need to compensate to eat polluted or dirty or poision fishes, ourselves bodies health will be bad. In long time, we need have high chance to pay medical expenditure when we are old. So, pollution case may be one good example to explain how and why human foolish behavior may influence ourselves future need to compensate serious medical loss.

All of these human foolish behavior will bring pollution to global ocean. On consequently, we will need to compensate to eat polluted or dirty or poison fished , ourselves bodies health will be bad. In long time, we will have high chance to pay medical expenditure, when we are old. So, pollution case may be one good example to explain how and why human ourselves intellectual or foolish behaviors may influence future long time economic loss or economic growth or recession in micro and micro economic view.

On another water pollution aspect hand, if we often keep rubbish to sea, oil exploration processing pollutes ocean and ships' gas pollute ocean, then fishes will eat polluted food and drink dirty water, due to fishes will eat polluted food and drink dirty sea water because the global ocean is polluted seriously.

In fact, because human only consider how to buy boats to carry on any leisure water activities, or catches cruises to travel on the sea. Also, oil manufacturers only consider any where to find oil exploratin places to manufacture oil products from ocean, when their pol exploration processes can plooute ocean. Consequently, global fishes drink polluted water or eat direty food. They will have poison. So, human will have high chance to eat poison fishes.

Otherwise, such as pollutin case, it can infuence inflation or deflation. Consequently, the reason indicates supply and demand theory. If air pollution is serious, then we will consider health issue, global cars demand number may be influenced to reduce, when global cars number demand will reduce, global car prices and supply number will need to change to fall down in order to attract or persuade global car consumers choose to make car purchase decision.

Hence, global car manufacture number and car price will be influenced to reduce, due to global air pollution issue. Consequently, deflation will occur because when the country citizen usually does not spend much extra saving money to buy car expensive goods. Money value will be low. Otherwise, if global cair pollution is not serious, human considers to buy cars to enjoy driving leisure lives. So, global car demand is influenced to increase , also global car price will also influenced to increase.

Consequently, gobal human will choose to buy cars to drive. Due to we accept to spend extra saving to buy expensive car goods. Car sale price and supply may be influenced to rise up. Money value is influenced to reduce. Inflation may be influenced, due to global car consumers number increases, we would not have extra money to spend easily. Car expensive goods expenditure influences our spending habit to avoid to make car purchase decision more easily. So, human intellectual or foolish activities may bring inflation or deflation consequency in possible indirectly in macro economic view.

On conclusion, above pollution case explain that how and why human intellectual or foolish economic behaviors may bring inflation or deflation consequency as wll as economic growth or recession consequency as well as any goods demand and supply increasing or decreasing consequency. It implies that human behavior may have indirect relationship to influence any goods demand and supply number to either increase or decrease result as well as any goods price will be influenced to increase or decrease in micro and macro economic view. Hence, Human foolish behavior is depended on social enjoyment need more or material social supply more because human needs to raise enjoyment feel , so we will choose to do foolish behavior, e.g. air pollution, when many people choose to buy cars to drive to replace catch public transport. So, such as car market, it depends on car demand number more than car supply number absolutely in demand and supply view.

The relationship between social change and human behavior

Why does economic changes may influence human individual behavioral change? I shall attempt to indicate shopping behavior and staying at home behavior to explain their case and effect relationsip as below:

Human behavior can be influenced by economic change or economic change can be influenced by human behavior? Why does recession may influence consumers reduce shopping desire? In social recession suitation, it is possible that many people lose jobs suddenly, due to businessmen lose many customers. They need to make decision to reduce employees number in order to continue to keep businesses. Consequently, many firms (organizations) their employees may lose jobs. When they have much time, due to lose jobs, they will feel to avoid to spend too much time and money to go to shopping often. Many losing jobs people, they will often stay at homes. So, they will reduce time to go to shopping, then non essential products won't their preferable choice purchase products. Hence, recession will change many losing jobs people their shopping or consumption desires to avoid to buy non essential products often . Usually when economic boom, many people have jobs to do because consumers number must increase when many people have jobs to do. Then, many people can accept to spend money to buy non essential products often. Many people feel spend time to go to shopping can satisfy their purchase of any kinds of new products useful psychology or desire. So, recession is one good example to explain it can influence many people do not like often to leave homes to go to shopping easily. Many people like to stay at homes, becaue they feel worry about spending too much shopping time when they leave homes. Their staying home time is one good negative shopping behavior example. So, economic change may influence human individual behavior changes , they have direct cause and efect relationship in behavioral economic view.

May human behavior influence economic change? Is it possible that human behavior may bring the country social economic change in macro economic or micro behavioral economic view ? I shall indicate publishing industry example. Do you feel that if there are many students feel learning is very important when they read many books or many of students feel interesting to read or they have reading new books in habit, then it is possible that the country will have many students like to spend time to go to any book shops to choose the books, they feel that they can help they learn new knowledge.

Then the country will increase students number, they often spend time to visit any one book shop every week. Their visiting book shops behavior which may become their habits. So, the country will increase students number, they often spend time to visit book shops. Also, it implies that visiting book shops behaviors may be their behavioral habits.

So, when the country has many students often spend time to visit book shops , their visiting book shops behaviors may help any one book shop to raise books sale chance. So, the country's student individual often visiting book shop behaviors, their habitual visiting book shops behaviors must may assist help any one book shop to increase books sale number absolutely.

Consequently, any one book shop , its books sale bumber must be influenced to increase to increase because the country will have many students like or feel need visit book shops habit in order to choose any suitable books to buy to read at home in order to raise themselves learning effort. When the country has many bok shops often have many students visit their book shops, then their books sale number may be influenced to increase. It explain why student individual visiting book shop behavior may help any one book shop sale number increases also. So, visiting shops products sale number is depended on online products supply number, if online products supply number increases, then it may cause many customers choose to buy the kind of products from online webstore. So, any shop products sale number will depend on onlint products supply number in supply and demand view.

CHAPTER FOUR

Human social demand and supply relationship

How human productive behavior may influence economic development

May any country which citizen behavior assist themselves country development? It is one cause and effect economic question. I mean that if the country itself citicen can not concentrate mind or energy to choose to do one kind of industry in order to let themselves country can bring the most benefit, then whether the counry itself economy can bring the most serious economic benefit. I shall attempt to indicate these countries themselves indistry choice to explain whether these countries themselves citizen productive behavior may help themselves countries to achieve the largest economic benefits. I shall indicate as below:

New Zealand farmer individual wine productive behavior

For New Zealand country example, this country concerns itself effort is foucs on farming agricultural aspect. So, this country has many farmers concentrate on farming agricultural aspect. May New Zealanders choose to spend time to produce different kinds of wines, e.g. wine or red grape wine is for the people are eating meat, or they are eating dinner.

When these New Zealanders their behaviors choose to do farming or agriculture to grow and produce different kinds of taste of white or red grape wine drinking products job. Themselves grape agriculture behavior will influence these New Zealanders themselves, they can learn how to improve different kinds of grape wine drinking products in order to achieve every kinds of white or read grape wines taste improving aim during their white or red grape producing process.

Why can New Zealander every individual white or read grape wine producers improve their white or read grape wine taste more easily? In behavioral economic view, it can explain that why any one New Zealander white or read grape wine producer can be encouraged or excited or persuaded to concentrate nervous and energy and effort to learn how to improve their white or red grape wine products easily.

In fact, New Zealand is one agricultural food export country. It has good natural environment resource , e.g. land, seed to provide any one farmer to produce themselves any kinds of agricultrual food products, e.g. fruit, or wine food products. Because New Zealanders know themselves country has enough natural resource . So, in common, many New Zealanders choose to attempt to do farming agricultural jobs in order to export themselves any kinds of fruit or meat or wine products to overseas or sell to domestic in order to earn profit.

So, when these New Zealand farmers number has been increasing every year. This country farmers will feel themsleves competition between this New Zealand farmers themselves are serious due to they may feel New Zealanders choose to do agriculture businesses in order to export themselves different kinds of farming food to overseas or sell to local to earn profit.

Hence, when many New Zealand farmers feel that farmers number has been increasing every year. They will feel themselves competition is serious. They must need to spend much time and nervous and effort to research what method is the best how to produce the best taste of white or red grape wine products in order to let local or overseas wine buyers to choose to buy his/her producing white or read grpae products to drink.

Hence, in competition psychological view, may influence many New Zealand white or reaad wine producers had been beginning to change their learning behavior on researching what method is the best in order to produce the best quality of taste red or white wine products to sell in order to attract overseas or local white or read grape wine drinkers to choose to buy his/her wine products. Their behavior will focus on learning how to raising or improving white or read grape wine taste method more than only focus on producing a large number white or red grape wine products. They believe wine quality is more important to compare wine producing number. So, New Zealand wine producers themselves wine producers behaviors have been changing on concentrating on researching wine quality method aspect more then wine producing number aspect in behavioral economic view.

America high technological productive behavior

For America example, US is one high technological country, it owns many high technological knowledge talent inventors, e.g. computer science inventors. Hence, US must attract many diferent countries owning high technological computer inventors choose to go to US to develop their computer science profession career. Also, it seems that when many computer science inventors or professions choose to go to US to develop themselves computer science new career. In behavioral economic view, due to their leaving themselves countries choice, which may bring influence themselve country job behaviors need to be changed. They must need to adapt US new live. Because they will forgive their past computer science job. These computer science professionals need to spend time to adapt US new lives. They " past computer science job behaviors" will need to be changed to their new US any computer employer's new computer science job model.

Because their traditional computer science jobs needed to be forgot in their themselves countries. They will feel their old computer science job knowledge and behavior needed to change in order to let their US any one new of computer company employer feels satisfactory to accept their new working behavior in any one US computer organization.

So, on the other hand, many US computer company employer will feel that they must need time to accept any one new overseas computer science professions their working behaviors, their working attitude daily, because these foreign comouter science professional, their past computer working behaviors and working attitude must be different to US domestic computer science professions.

In behavioral economic view, these overseas computer science professions, their working behaviors and attitude must be needed to change in order to adapt any one US new computer company itself domestic or local computer science professional stafs themselves daily working behaviors and attitude because these overseas and local computer science professionals must need to team work together.

In behavioral economic view, it is only one way that foreign computer science professionals must need to change themselves past country traditiona daily working behaviors and attitude in order to cooperate with these US local computer science professionals in teams more easily.

Consequently, if these foreign compute science professionals can change their past working behaviors and attitude to let any one US local computer science professional feels to cooperate with them easily in short time. Then, the US computer company itself whole computer professional teams themselves efficiencies will be influenced to raised or improved by the changing past working attitude and working behaviors of these foreign computer science professionals. So, in behavioral economic view, only if US any one computer company hopes itself computer teams themselves efficiency can be raised or improved when it decides to employ foreign computer science professionals and US domestic computer science professionals. They need to work in teams together. They must need to let these foreign computer science professionals to know how to change their working behaviors and attitude to let their domestic computer science professionals feel easy to work together. Then, the US computer company itself whole team efficiency must be rasied or improved easily in short time.

- China share market investing behavior

For China share market example, economic development depends on financial market. Because if many Chinese have interest to invest to carry on shares buying and selling activities in orde to learn how to earn shares interest and share profit when the China shareholder can make decision to sell himself/herself shares in the the high price, then he/she can earn money when he/she can sell the China company's shares in the high sale share price position.

If China has many Chinese like to spend time to carry on investing shares activities. Themselves shares buying and selling behaviors will influence China has many companies can increase fund from many Chinese shareholders in order to have enough money to expand or develop themselves businesses in China in long term.

Consequently, when China can have many Chinese like to attempt to carry on buying and selling shares investing behaviors in China share market. Themselves buying and selling shares behaviors can help many Chinese companies have effort to increase enough money or capital in order to continue to do their businesses in long term absolutely. So, it explains why when many Chinese become shareholders , they can assist China will have many companies continue to develop their businesses if many Chinese like to carry on shares buying and selling investing behaviors in long time in China financial investment market nowadays in behavioral economic view.

Why has any individual country have many people invest share behavior which can influence the country's macro consumption desire?

I shall apply shares market buying and selling investment behavior to explaiin why shares investment behavior which may impact the country's overal consumption desire as below:

In behavioral economic view, I assume that when the coutry has many people have interest to attempt to carry on shares buying and selling investment behavior, then their frequent shares buying and selling behaviors which may bring negactive consumption desire or shopping desire of these shares investors their consumer behavior.

The reason is simple, when the country has many share buyers number suddenly been increasing rapidly. Consequently, these large group share investors must need to spend much time to research any kinds of company shares variations, whether when their share prices will rise up of fall down in order to achieve buying the company's shares in the lowest price and selling the company's shares in the highest price level in order to earn profit.

Basic on this reason, they must need to spend much extra time to research share prices changing behavior every day, e.g. one working person will wait to leave his/her job, after he/she can spend time to gather data to research the day's share price changing behavior after dinner. So, the working person's right time may be his/her share price market research behavior. Before he/she may spend his/her night time to go to shopping after dinner, but nowadays, he/she will fogive to do his/her shopping behavior before dinner or after dinner at hight sometime. He/she will make decision to spend much night time to turn on computer to click on share market website to research his/her share purchase choice to investigate whether his/her share price whether it rises up or falls down at the moment in order to make his/her share buying or selling decision at ever night time.

I mean the when the country has many people are share investors, their shares investment behavioral spenging time which will influence many shops lose customers at might often because the country will have many people feel need to spend night time to turn on computer or watch television to investigate share price variation. So, the country will have many people / share investors choose to stay at home in order to carry on share price variation investigation behavior, they need to listen share market update news from radios or watch the share market update news from computer or TV at home every night. Consequenly, they must reduce times to leave themselves homes at night. So, their shopping behavior also will be reduced. Because these share investors feel need to spend time to investigate share price variation news at homes which can bring economic benefits (high opportunity benefits) when they choose to forgive to leave homes to go to shopping times (opportunity cost) every night.

On conclusion, it seems that when the country has many people are share investors, then their share price investigating behavior may bring negative shopping emotion at night. Consequently, the country's any one shop may lose many customers from this share investor consumer group in behavioral economic view. Hence, when the country's share investors number had been increasing rapidly, it will influence any shops lose many customers from this share investing customer group at night frequenly in short time, even long time in behavioral economic view, because their shopping desires or shopping emotion will be brought negative feeling when they make decisions to spend much time to listen radios or watch TV or computers share price update nes at night. Hence, share market will bring negative impact to influence consumer shopping desire or negative shopping emotion in behavioral economic view.

CHAPTER FIVE

Technology demand and supply relationship

Can technology influence human shopping behavioral change?
Nowadays, technological development has reached mature stage, whether technological mature stage may bring positive or negative shopping emotion influence to global consumers. I shall aplly internet inventin or ecommerce shopping channel tool to explain whether internet technology can bring postive or negative influence to global consumer behavior in behavioral economic view.

Internet is a good technological tool, it brings e-commerce business chance. In fact, commonly, global has have many businessmen choose to use internet channel to carry on their products transactions between global online-buyers and their electronic websites. So, global many shoppers had begun to feel online shopping is more convenient to compare visiting shops shopping. Their shopping behaviors have been changed from internet technological tool. Global has many shoppers choose to buy any products from any overseas or local businessmen their web stores. They only need to spend time to find any businessmen their webstores to choose the most suitable products to pay visa to buy from their webstores. at homes. So, in general, global had have may shoppers had changed their shopping behaviors from visiting shops to visiting webstores at homes often.

So, it seems that internet technological tool had influenced global many shops disappear, but internet webstores will be replaced their actual shops on streets. Some of businessmen either they choose webstores to replace shops or choose websotes and shops both or still keep shops only. Hence, internet tool influences global businessmen have three kinds of products sale channels to let globa local and overseas consumers to choose how to buy their products.

However, in fact, many of global shoppers, youngers and olders had begun to accept to buy any products from webstores. They feel to spend time to leave homes to visit shops , their shopping behaviors will be wasted time to not essential part to their daily lives. Hence, since internet technological invention, it had changed many consumers their traditional visiting shops shopping habit to change to buying products from webstores channel.

However, on the one hand, internet creates webstores ecommerce shopping channel to let global many consumers do not need to leave homes to go to shopping. It brings negative visiting shops shopping emotion to global general consumers nowadays. But on the other hand, it also brings positive visiting internet webstores shopping emotion to global general consumer nowadays. So, it seems that global many consumers feel that they often do not need to spend much time to go out shopping. Many global consumers feel convenient and enjoy to choose any products to buy from different internet webstores, when the online buyer chooses the most suitable product, he she only needs to pay visa card to buy the product from the online seller's webstore conveniently at home.

Hence, online shopping can bring economic benefit to online buyers, e.g. avoiding walking time or spending transport fare to visit the shop to go to shopping, shortening or reducing shopping time to do another important matter.

On conclusion, global many consumers began feel online shopping can bring more economic benefits on shortening shopping time, avoiding transport fare spending aspect. So, online shopping will be popular shopping behavior for future long time. It may encourage global many shoppers can make rapid shopping decision in short time in order to carry on any products buying transaction to global any one online shopper in short time easily in behavioral economic view. So, global many businessmen had begun to build themselves one attraction webstore in order to persuade different countries consumers to choose to click themselves webstores from internet channel to buy any kinds of products in short time easily.

So, internet technology had changed consumers traditional shopping behaviors to build positive online shopping emotion as well as raise online sellers' any products sale chance easily in behavioral economic view.

Why and how human behavior may influence the country's economic growth or recession?

When one country has many people choose to do the same matter for one period, whether their behavior may influence the country's pvera;

economic growth or recession . I shall attempt to indicate cases toexplain their relationship as below:

For flowing rubblish behavioral case example, do you feel that when the country has many people often flow rubblish on the streets, instead of their flowing rubblish behavior may bring streets dirty? But, their flowing rubblish behavior may explain that this country has people may have enough money to buy food to ear, or enough cloths to wear, enough bottles of water to drink, even they may have enough money to buy new television, radio, refrigeraters , washing machines, desktops or laptops electronic home products from old to new to use in order to satisfy their living needs. So, when they flow old electronic home products, their flowing old home electronic products behaviors may seem that they have enough money to buy other new home electronic products to replace old home electronic products to use at homes.

However, it seems thaat this country ought have many people have jobs to do. So, many of them, they can easy to make purchase decison to flow any old home electronic products and buy any new home electronic products to use . Because this country has many people have jobs to do. So, they can often not use old home electonic products to become rubblishs to flow on streets after they had bought any kinds of new home electronic homes.

In fact, it also implies that this country's economy grows rapidly. So, many businesses can glow up rapdly. When they expanded their businesses, they must need to increase employees number in order to let they help themselves to raise productivity or serve their clients absolutely. So, when the country has many businesses can grow up, it seems that its economy must be better or it is improved to compare past. Due to many different kinds of home electronic products had been often bought to use by this country people in this period. So, this country's any streets can be observed that expensive electronic home products were flowed on streets anywhere. then, this country will have many electronic home products sellers can sell their home electronic products very easily. When this country has many people can find any kinds of jobs to do easily. So, due to unemploymen rate had been decreasing.

In behavioral economic view, as this many electronic home products rubblish country case, we can observe this country may have many people have jobs to do. So, consumption number has been increased long time. So, cheap food, or expensive home electronic products may be rubblish on any streets. This country's people , their flowing rubblish behaviors may be explained that many of people have enough jobs to do, so they have ability to buy any good taste food to eat or buy any kinds of expensive electronic home products to use. So, this country's economy may be improved for this long period. So, in behavioral economic view, when this country can have many electronic home products rubblishs are flowed on anywherer in streets frequently. It seems that this country will have many people have jobs to do, so it causes they often change old home electronic products or replaced them easily, when they have enough income to spend to buy any kinds of new home electronic products to use at homes easily. Moreover, their flowing old electronic home products behaviors also indicate that this country has many people their salaries may be increased in possible from their emplyers. When this country can have many different kinds of home electornic products are sold. It means that this country's electronic home products needs or demand had been increasing, due to many people have jobs to do and income increases to excite their living of needs also improve. Consequently, this country may seem have better economic improvement. We can observe from this country's electronic home products rubblish increasing income in theis period.

On conclusion, this country ought experience economic growth at this period. So, " flowing expensive electronic home rubblish increasing number " may seem that this country's economic growth is rapidly in this period, due to many people have jobs to do as well as salaries increase in this period.

Technology how impacts human behavior changing?

Technology how influences human behavior to bring changing? For example, online share purchase and sale transaction from smart phone brings share investor can do share buying or selling transation in any where and any time conveniently, non manual driving auto vehicle, bring car owner feels comfortable and spends free time to do other matter, e.g. reading, listening mucis in himself or herself car freely. electrical energy vehicle can help car owner to reduce air polluton and it can brings the drivers do not feel drive long time in any journeys in order to avoid air pollution for environmental protection responsible car drivers in our societies. Thus, they will drive long time in any journeys when they can drive electronic energy cars to replace oil energy cars.

However, online technology can also bring consumers can choose to stay at homes to buy any things from seller individual online webstore conveniently. Such as online technology can bring shoppers do not need to spend much time to visit shops to buy any things. They can choose any kinds of products from any online sellers individual online webstores conveniently at homes. Online technology excite busy consumers can make purchase decision easily as well as it can help online sellers sell any kinds of products from internet easily.

In behavioral economic view, technology can change human behavior to be improved, it can let human feels comfortable, more free time ro use, rapid making any decisions, such as apply smart phones to make share purchase or sale transaction decision, online shopping decision, even travelling any where decision in short time, when the traveller finds the most cheap hotel accommodation room price and air ticket price frm any travel agent online tourism webstore, then the potential travel customer can follow the online hotel accommodation price and air ticket price data to make decision when to buy the air ticket from the airline travel agent or make decision when to prebook which hotel accommodation room to go to the country to travel from online travel agent tourism webstores. So, technology can encourage global any country travelers to make anywhere to trvel rapidly. If the traveler can find the country's general hotel rooms and airline tickets prices had been decreasing more sightly. The traveler may make travel decision to choose the country to travel in short time, then he/she can prebook the country;s any hotel room and airline ticket to pay by visa fraom the country's any hotel and airline travel agent webstores., before one week, even one month or more easily. Hence, online technology can also encourage traveler individual frequent travel times to be increased, due to global travelers can find any hotel rooms and airline tickets prices from internet conveniently at homes. They do not need to spend time to visit any airline travel agent to enquire travel choice country's hotel rooms prices and airline ticket prices. They can compare global travel of countries choices ' all hotels rooms and airline agents air tickets prices to make prebook airline seat and hotel room decision before one week, one month even six months early.

On conclusion, online technology can encourage global travelers can make travelling any where and when traveling time desicions easily. It can excite tourism industry develops in long time. Also, such as electricity cars invention can encourage environment protection car owners do car purchase decision easily, because they can choose to drive electronic energy cars to replace oil energy cars in order to avoid air pollution occurs easily. So, electronic cars can increase electronic car purchasrs number, due to many of environmental protection attitude of car owners can choose to drive electricity cars to bring air cleans, even non -manual driving cars can encourage lazy driving and free time driving car owners to choose to buy non-manual (artificial intelligent) cars to drive , because they can spend much free time to read, listen music or do any matters in themselves cars, they do not need to drive cars, robotic (AI) auto driving machine is such one non-manual driver to help them to drive themselves cars confidently. So, non-manual driving cars can attract lazy and enjoying free time driving car owners to choose to buy to replace traditional manual cars to drive easily. Moreover, online share transaction can help any share investors to make share buying and selling decision in short time easily. When they can apply smart phones technological tool to carry on share buying and selling activities easily. They can observe any share rising or falling price suitation from smart phones in any where any any time easily. So, smart phone technology can help global any shareholders to make share purchase and sale transaction easily. So, technology can encourage human makes decision in short time rapidly.

How and why employees behaviors may influence economy development?

In behavioral economy view,I believe the country's any organizational employees behavior may bring indirect relationship to influence the country's long term economic development. I shall indicate past manufacture industry social development period to explain their relationship. For many countries' past business activities had belonged to manufacturing industry, such as US, UK past before 1980 year, it focused on steel manufacturing and steel manufacturing related machine products. So, US, Uk developed countries manufacturing industries may be past main country's economic income sources. I assume US , UK past had one million number different kinds of industries. They ought had about seven houndred thousand number organizational businesses were belonged to manufactured industry. They may include:

Steel manufacturing and steel related machine manufacturing, e.g. vehicle manufacturing, home appliances, e.g. washing machine, television, radio, refrigerate cooler, heater, air condition etc. different kinds of different kinds of steel -related manufacturing machine, they were manufactured from US, UK steel machine manufacturers. So, US, Uk the other three hundred thousand number industry may be general service industry, e.g. hotel service, restaurent, cinema, public transport service, tourism lesiure , wine bar, supermarket etc. different kinds of non-manufacturing industries business organizations were operated in UK, US past before 1980 year.

So, in UK, US developed countries industry development history, they ought have high percentage of businesses belonged to steel related manufacturing machine and steel products. Also, in the past before 1980 year, US, Uk business employers , they employed many workers are manufacturing workers. They needed to spend long time to work in factories. They were skillful workers, and they are trained to manufacturing cars, washing machine, television, heater, etc. even steel itself different kinds of steel related products to prepare to deliver to their shops to sell to US, Uk local or overseas clients.

So, I believe that past UK, US ought employ many employees, they belonged to skillful manufacturing workers, manufacture increasing steel machine or steel related machine number of products rapidly daily. So, if UK, US had had many of these manufacturing factories owned high skillful workers, then their manufacturing steel-related machine or steel both kinds of products number must be influenced to raise rapidly. Consequently, their steel machine manufacturing products would been exported to overseas or would been sold to local both markets , they may be influenced to raise sale number. They (these manufacturing workers) needed to be trained to know how to manufactur these different kinds of machine products in the efficient teams and they ought to be trained to raise their efficiencies in order to shorten time to manufacturing many kinds of steel related manufacturing machine or steel itself products rapidly. So , if their efficiencies and manufacturing performance was improved, these US, UK any one manufacturing worker and their teams ought achieve raising productivities significantly.

Hence, when past UK, US manufacturing industry development period, if these two countries' any manufacturing factories could have many manufacturing workers could be trained to be skillful and proficient manufacturing workers. Then, in past every day to these factories workers, they ought help their steel or steel related manufacturing employers to raise any kinds of machine or steel products number in every team. So, when past in the manufacturing industry development, US, UK could have many factories' manufacturing workers themselves steel or steel related machine products manufacturing skill could be trained to to improve to any kinds of these machine or steel manufacuring products quality as well as their products number could be influenced to raise by themselves skillful improvement significantly every day.

Then, what would be influenced to occur to past UK, US manufacturing industry period? In behavioral economic view, when these two manufacturing industry developed countries, such as UK, US , if they had many factories workers can be trained to improve their skill in order to achieve any kinds of steel or steel-related machine products quality could be improved as well as products manufacturing number could be also increased absolutely.

In consequence, past UK and US both countries ought increase themselves any kinds of steel and steel related machine products number to be supplied to themselves local shops to let local clients to choose any one kind of machine manufacturing products to buy easily as well as they could also export to supply overseas any countries to buy their different kinds of steel or steel related machine products to let overseas steel or steel related manufacturing machine product buyers, they can have many of these different kinds of these steel or steel-related different kinds of manufacturing machine from UK and UK these both countries easily to compare other countries.

On conclusion, I believe that past US, and UK macro manufacturing industry income GDP would increase significantly. So, they would have good economic growth performance because when many of these manufacturing workers themselves manufacturing effort could be improved. So, it explained when employees manufacturing abilities can influence economic growth indirectly.

Robots invention whether they can help organizations to raise efficiencies or inefficiencies?

In behavioral economic view, in any organizations, when the organization hopes its worker teams can raise efficiencies , the organization may choose to increase more workers number and/or it can provide training to improve these workets themselves skills in order to raise their efficiencies. For one warehouse example, when the warehouse increases many goods , they are needed to delivered these goods from the shelves to the delivering destination locations. If this warehouse supervisors feel these workers themselves goods delivery speeds are slow, which is possible due to this warehouse's workers number is not enough. So, this warehouse supervisor ought increase workers number in order to increase their goods delivery speed in order to deliver goods from the shelves to every indicated goods delivery destination in order to let any one lorry driver can transport the right kinds of goods and ensure the accurate goods number to transport to any one client home rapidly.

However, if this warehouse supervisor planed to buy several warehouse goods delivery robots to assist these warehouse workers to find the right kinds of goods from shelves and then deliver to the right destination location in the warehouse. So, these warehouse orkers can concentrate on counting the accurate goods number and ensuring the right kinds of goods in order to prepare to let lorry drivers to transport these goods to these goods of buyers themselvers homes rapidly. Consequently, in the first step, robots can concentrate on finding th right goods from shelves and delivers them to the right goods transportation of location destination. Then, in the second step, these warehouse workers can concentrate on counting the accurate goods number and ensuring the right kinds of goods in order to prepare to put them to the lorry. Consequently, when warehouse robots and warehouse workers can cooperate to work together, the most important, robots, can deal on finding the right kinds of goods and deal on delivering the accurate number of goods of job duty as well as these warehouse workers can only concentrte on counting the right kinds of goods number in order to avoid it has none any mistake of wrong kinds of goods and inaccurate goods of delivery number to be transported to the lorry and to deliver to any one buyer's home.

So, it seems that warehouse robots ought help any one warehouse worker to raise himself efficiency and avoid goods delivery of mistake occurrence easily as well as their help to warehouse workers that can let any one goods buyer feels their goods can be delivered to their homes rapidly. Moreover, warehouse robots can also help these warehouse workers to raise efficiencies because warehouse robots can help them to shorten goods delivery time between any one shelf and any one goods delivery destination of location in the warehuse because robots may help them to find the right kinds of goods from the right shelf in the short time. So, any one worker does not need to spend long time to seek anywhere is the right shelf location for the kind of goods when the kind of goods are needed to deliver to the buyer's home from lorry. Warehouse robots can help them to do this aspect of " finding the goods from the right shelf in short time job duty". So, any one warehouse worker only needed tospend less time to do the counting of any right kind of goods number and ensuring the right kind of goods job duty. Consequently, this warehouse 's any one worker, his any one kind of goods delivery time may be reduced, because robots' assistance and they may have more confidence to avoid mistake to deliver the wrong number of goods and/or the wrong kind of goods to any one goods buyer's home.

On conclusion, it seems that warehouse robots ought may help any one warehouse worker to raise efficiency for any one team in the warehouse as well as the warehouse any one supervisor does not need to spend much time to observe any one worker individual performance for " goods delivery job duty aspect" because their goods delivery job duty that had been replaced to do by these several warehouse robots. Robots can achieve the more accurate of right kinds of goods and the right number of goods delviery job performance to compare any one of human warehouse worker themselves right kinds of goods of delivery and right number of goods of delivery job performance. So, when robots can participate to cooperate with this warehouse's any one worker to do their goods of delivery job duty in this warehouse every day. Then, robots can raies any one of supervisor individual confidence in order to let they do not need to spend time to observe any one of worker individual whose goods of delivery job performane. They can concentrate on supervising any one worker whose goods transport to lorry in the final step in order to avoid to deliver wrong goods number and / or wrong kind of goods to any one goods buyer's home every day. Consequently, this warehouse's overall teams of their delviery of goods performance many be improved by robotss' participatin to goods of delivery task as well as this warehouse's oveall teams themselves efficiencies may be influenced to raise by robots' goods of delivery task participation.

Why social behavior may influence organizational strategy needs to be changed ?

Why any organizations need to know whether nowadays social behaivor how has been changing in order to implement the kind of the most right strategy to achieve the profit aim pursue in possible. I shall indicate nowadays ecommerce or online, customer shopping behavior to explain above question concerns they ought have close relationship between social behavior and organizational strategic choice or organizational behavioral changing need.

On nowadays ecommerce business, or online shopping model, this kind of shopping model in global many young and old age consumers like to apply internet tool to choose any country sellers website stores in order to stay at home to buy any kinds of products from themselves webstores in global

societies.
In fact, online shopping model had been popular for long time above to twenty years. Most of global sellers will make decision to design themselves webstores in order to attract global many online buyers to choose to buy their products from themselves webstores. So, it seems that social consumers purchase behaviors had been changed to online shopping from internet invention.
Hence, social consumers purchase behavioral changes may influence any organizations' strategies need to be changed from visiting shops purchase strategy model to online purchase strategy model, if the seller still concentrate on concentrate on considerate how to design itelf , but neglects to considerate how to design itself webstore, e.g. how to design attract product photos to put on itself webstore, how to arrange sale price information location to be putted on webstore and visa card payment location on itself webstore in order to let any one online buyer can feel very easier to buy itself any kinds of products from itself webstore. Then, its potential online buyers will be influenced to increase number when they can find this online seller itself any kinds of products photes and every kinds of product sale price information and visa card payment channel locations easily from itself webstore.
So, it implies that nowadays any one seller ought need to design one webstore to let any one online overseas and domestic consumers can have chance to click itself webstore to choose any one kind of product to buy conveniently when he/she does not hope to leave him/her home to go to shop, because nowadays social shopping behaviors had been influenced to change when internet invention, them it gives another online purchase method to replace visiting shops purchase method to global any one buyer in nowadays societies.
So, if nowadays any one seller still concentrate on how to design itself shop display in order to put any kinds of product on shelf in order to let any one visiting shop customer to find the kind of product to buy, but it neglects to change to choose to pursue another new technological shopping method, such as webstore purchase method in order to implement effective strategy to design the most right webstore as well as in order to attract global overseas and local consumers to find itself webstore easily from website and find its any one kind of product phots and sale price and visa card payment button in order to choose to buy itself any kinds of products in the short time. Consequently I believe that the seller will lose many customers from

overseas and local when its other same or similar product sellers choose to design themselves webstores in order to let global any one product buyer can buy themselves any one kind of product when they can pay visa card to buy their products from them webstores conveniently when they stay at home habitly. Then, the seller will lose many global potential customers in long time.

On conclusion, in behavioral economic view, any consumer behavioral social changing, which will influence any in order to avoid customers number loses significantly . In future time, organizations need to make rapid decision in order to implement the most reasonable and the most useful strategy in order to avoid global potential customers number reduces or lose them in long time. So, social behavioral changing environment ought influence any global organizations need to decide how to change themselves strategies in order to avoid customers loses significantly in future time.

How and why human behavior may influence economic growth or recession?

May ourselves daily behaviors influence our global societial continue economic growth or recession? Do they have cause and effect close relationship between human behaviors and global economic growth or recession? I shall apply behavioral economic theory to analyze and explain whether ourselves daily behaviors and our global societial economic growth or recession which have close cause and effect relationship as below:

Every country itself economic development must depend on any business activities, otherwise, any kinds of business activities must need ourselves business activities or behaviors in order to achieve any business activities as well as achieve the country's overall economic development in macro view. However, any country's overall business activites or behaviors which must depend on any kinds of individual businessmen, themselves employees daily working behavior or activity or performance in order to help them to attract or increase many clients number to acieve " earning profit" aim. So, it seems that any individual business, itself overall every department individual working behavior is one main factor to influence the company's overall business performance.

For agricultural fruit and meat food farming industry example, such as New Zealand is a farming main target industry country. It had had many New Zealanders were daily themselves own farming businesses for many years. Their farming businesses include growing fruit, sheep, cow, pig pork, meat etc. food sale business. If the New Zealand farmer owned a large size farming land, then he will choose either growing fruit or feeding sheeps, pigs, cows to be meat to to transport to New Zealand supermarkets to help them to sell to their farmers meet to New Zealanders in order to earn profit. Thus, if the New Zealand farmer owned large size of farming lands, then he needs to employ many farming employees (farming workers) to help him to carry on farming business daily tasks, e.g. picking up friuts, feeding pigs, cows, sheeps to eat food daily. These daily farming jobs are very important to influence this New Zealand farmer's meats or fruits sale number whether they can be easy or diffcult to sell in New Zealand supermarkets , if these farming workers can own encough farming knowledge or skill to know how to pick up fruits method and make judgement to know whether it is right time to pick up the kind of fruits from the trees , as well as know how feed this pigs, sheeps, cows to eat food in order to let they are better health. Consequently, their farming behaviors which can let these animals can provide the best taste and enough meat from these animals to let New Zealander to buy to eat from New Zealand any one supermarket. Even these New Zealand farming workers can know whether the kinds of fruits, e.g. oranges, apples, gapes etc. fruits whether they ought be picked up from the trees at the right time. Consequently, they can make judgement to decide to pick up any kinds of the best taste fruits to let any one New Zealander to buy to eat from any one supermarket in New Zealand. Otherwise, if they do not make judegement to know whether the kind of fruit ought not be picked up because they still need longer time to continue grow up to increase fruit size and better taste from the trees in order to let any one fruit buyer can feel better taste when they eat this kind of fruit later. If they can buy this kind of fruit to eat later, then this New Zealand farmer's his fruit buyers can buy the best taste of this kind of fruit to eat from an yone supermarket in New Zealand. Consequently, many New Zealand supermarkets will choose to buy any kinds of fruits from this farmer fruit supplier when they feel this farmer's fruits can provide more better taste fruits to compare other farmers' fruits.

Thus, due to New Zealand is one farming main income source country. It's any kinds of fruits and meats need to be export to overseas to sell , instead of local sale. It's GDP percent is very high to whole country 's overall income source. So, any one New Zealand farmer individual and any one farming worker individual working behavior will influence its economy whether it is influenced to grow or recession possible. Moreover, it also seems that farming workers' farming knowledge and skill will influence themselves farming daily activities to achieve the aim of the number of increase or decrease to any kinds of fruits whether they are better taste or the number of increase of decrease to any kinds of meats whether they are better taste to supply to any one New Zealand fruit or meat buyers to eat from any one New Zealand supermarket. So, it implies that any one New Zealand farming worker individual farming behavior may influence any kinds of fruits or any kinds of meat taste because they are transported to any one supermarket to sell in New Zealand.

Consequently, if New Zealans had many farmers can teach god farming knowledge and skill to let their any one farming workers know how to decide judgement to decide when it is right time to pick up any kinds of fruits from trees , or how to grow them on soil in order to let they can grow rapidly. Then, many different kinds of fruits can be provided to let any one New Zealanders can eat the best taste of fruits when their fruits are supplied to any one New Zealand supermarkets. Even, if they knew how to feed foods to pigs, cows, sheeps to eat daily. Then they can be more health and they can provide the best taste of meats to let any one New Zealanders can buy their meats from any one New Zealand supermarkets. Moreover, their fruits and meats can be transported to overseas to let any one country fruits or meats buyers can choose any kinds of New Zealand meats and fruits to buy to eat from themselves countries supermarkets. Then, many overseas fruit and meat buyers will perfer to choose New Zealand any kinds of fruits or meats to buy to compare other countries fruits or meats to buy when they go to any one local supermarkets.

On conclusion, it seems that New Zealand farming workers themselves farming behavior may influence their farming employers any kinds of fruits or meats sale number and income because their farming task behaviors must influence whether their fruits or meats taste are the better taste or worse taste to compare their other local farmers (the farmer competitors) whose fruits or meats taste. If tthe farmer's any one farming worker can be trained to learn how to know to feed animals skill and when is the most right time to pick up any kinds of fruits from trees or how to grow them on the soil methods. Due to these farming worker individual farming behavior may influence his different finds of fruits and meats sale number to be increase or decrease, so these any one New Zealand farmer must need to depend on any one farming worker whose farming working methods, if their farming working behaviors can be the best to influence any kinds of fruits to grow rapid or any kinds of pigs, cows, sheeps animals grow up rapidly , then their sale number may be increase significantly and their taste can be improved to let any New Zealand or overseas meat or fruit buyer to buy to eat to feel from any one New Zealand or overseas supermarkets, then New Zealand's agriculture industry must be influenced to increase. In the world, any one fruit or meat buyer must choose to buy New Zealand's fruit and meat to eat in prefer to compare other countries' fruits and meats. So, New Zealand's GDP may be influenced to raise from any one New Zealand farming worker individual farming working behaviors. It seems that New Zealand farmer fruit and meat sale number is depended on their eatting consumers demand more than their meat and fruit supply because if these NZ farmers can apply high technology method to grow good taste fruit or feed good taste meat to let global eatting customers to feel, their demand will increase, then NZ farmers will need to increase good taste fruit and good taste meat supply number to satisfy global meat and fruit eatting customer taste need.

CHAPTER SIX

What factors influence oil price changes

How the price of oil changes influences global tourism industry growth or recession?

In macro-economic view, sudden mid and long term oil price shock can influence global torusim industry growth or recession. For example, a oil price of US$180 per barrel was considered only a few years ago, now this has a realistic scenario to which all plaers in the T&T sector have to adapt. At such a high level, the price of oil will become even more critical to almost every part of the tourism value chain. Although, weak global demand, caused by global economic recesson, resulted in a steep oil price decline to US$45 per barrel by the fourth quarter of 2008 in the past low oil price occurrence history, this won't change the mid to long -term oil forecast.

In fact, the past oil price occurrence history of the dramatic structural had changed a high price imposed on airlines, travelers, and destination countries, all of which will have to navigate through times of shifting or even declining travel demand. I assume that a high oil price scenario is assumed in the long term in order to highlight the changes , such a senario would mean for consumer behavior and the competitiveness of several destinations.

Low oil price in the 1970 and early 1980 did not bring significant growth of international air travel, but its growth has been strongest between 1980 and 2004, a period with stable and relatively moderate oil prices. Also, the rapid development of the low-cost carrier business model in the 1990s further fueled air travel growth by capturing tourism leisure demand , such as weekend leisure travel to cities using mostly secondary airports in any big area countries, such as UK, US . However, the tourism growth is whole influenced by high oil prices, due to oil price had been continue rising in possible.

Basis of oil is shortage supply product, oil is assumed to be the main energy source for the aviation sector for the nest 30 years. Although, second-generation biofuels seem to be on the horizon, the economics as well as the production scalability and aviation biofuel shortage will be a main challenge to airline industry. So, I assume that oil price will continue rise up, if there have none any aviation biofuel can be reflected to oil to use for air plane energy.

Until 2004, the only factors to have affected air travel growth, negatively were in external shocks , such as 9/11, causes catching air plane crisis or US regional geopolitical conflicts. It brings some travelers feel fear to go to US travel, as well as until recently 2019, human mouth disease can influence air to have disease to anyone from mouth. So, global travelers number had been continue decreasing, because they are fear to get disease by air when many themselves every stranger travelers are sitting on the without windows air planes. Although, mouth human and air disease and US 9/11 air attack both matters may influence oil price falls effect, because air planes flying times will reduce. They won't need frequent to fly, to cause aviation oil energy need reduce. Consequently, oil price will decrease, due to travelers number reduces and air planes flying times are also influenced to reduce. (oil demand decreases cause oil price decrease). Although, air lines ' cost will also be influenced reduce, but oil price decrease can not bring travelers number increase , when air ticket price reduce because global many leisure and business trip travelers feel fear to catch air planes frequently when human mouth air disease occured in 2019. So, oil price decreases can not grow up tourism industry growth or rise tourism income.

However, the obvious impact of a high oil price is an increase in the operating costs of airline. Moreover, fuel cost as a percentage of airline operating costs vary significantly based on the length of the flight. The longer the flight, the higher the fuel costs as a percentage of the airline operating cost. So, from an online's perspective, long -hauel flights represent the most criticial challenge to profitable operation because the share of fuel on these flights, compared with other cost items, is largest, because of the unfacorable fuel economics, due to fuel costs even at high-load factors. For example, Thai airways dropped its non-stop Bongkok to US flights in the summer of 2008 for commercial reasons, because fuel reached operating cost levels of 55 percent on this route, a cost burden that could not be passed on to their customers. So, the estimated price elacticity of passengers demand at this Bongkok to US flights route is high, if Thai Airways rises less air ticket price, it will influence many travelers to choose other airlines to catch air plan to fly. Hence, due to Thai Airways can not make decision to rise air ticket price, because it believes that it will lose many travelers, so it only chooses to drop this non-stop Bongkok to US flights to avoid fuel cost rising economic loss.

However, although micro and macro economic theories may also that oil price variable or change, it may influence global tourism income. But, recently, on 2019, human mouth and air diseases, it can influence global individual leisure and business trip travelers feel fear to catch air plans to avoid their bodies get this kind of death sickness when they sit in the no fresh air supplying air planes. They feel that they reduce leisure travelling flying times or business trip flying times with strange travelers to sit in crowd air planes together. Then, they must many avoid human moth and air disease to avoid death crisis. Hence, in this global human mouth and air diseases threat environment occurrence, even oil price sudden reduces to low price, it brings airline's cost reduces and air ticke price reduces. However, when air ticket price reduce to be very cheaper, it can not still attract global many leisure or business trip travelers to buy air tickets to fly frequently. Why does air ticket reduction, it can not attract many leisure or businee trip travelers to buy air ticket to fly ? The main reason is because human mouth and air disease influences global many travelers feel fear to catch air planes frequently. In psychological view, this kind of human mouth and air sickness will bring long time negative influence to global traveles do not want to catch air planes for business trips or travelling leisure frequently. So, it implies that oil price changing to influence air ticket price reduction factor ought not main factor to influence tourism income. It may include traveler individual negative emotion psychological factor, such as human mouth and air disease or 2019 9/11 attack both cases, they can influence global travelers feel fear to catch air planes to fly to avoid death threat. So, oil changing price ought not be only one absolute main factor to influence global tourism income significantly.

On conclusion, in economic view, it seems that oil chang price may have indirect or direct relationship to influence tourism income, instead of some unpredicted external environment factors influence, such as US 9/11 attack crisis and human mouth and air disease factors, they may be main factors to influence travellers number to reduce in non-economic external unpredicted environment view.

How did First World War influence Europe economy and tourism industry declines ?

Can wars bring either advantages or disadvantages or both to impact our economy growth ?In history, I feel that international war can influence any country's economy development has either positive or negative impact in possible.

On the inflationary hand, for the First World War economy growth influence example, in the First World War and since most notably the German hyperinflation of the 1920 year, this type of monetary regime shows a far smaller tendency towards inflation. In the First World War period, volatility of inflation and output were higher in the short run. So, First World War had little negative impact to influence world inflation in the war period. However, in the First World War period, the supply of money was determined not by the rates of economic growth only, but by the amount of available gold and could not be adjusted in response to economic needs. So, new sources of gold would increase money supply and inflation and decrease interest rates , the opposite of what modern central banks would do to provide stable economic growth in First World War. So, it explained that the First World War occurrence caused the change from non-inflationary to inflationary long term development. Thus, it seems First World War brings more money supply and gold supply to stable economic growth in the future long term period.

On the labor productivity influence hand, leaving monetary issues aside, the First World War created the working time intellectual mood to change labor productivity, it would be a 15-18 hours working week for more enlightened leisure to Europe labors. Some prominent modern economists on the accuracy of the predictions on GDP growth per capital was remarkably accurate given to be fallen down that it was made at the time when economy growth theory did not even exist in the First World War period. Thus, it seems First World War also causes working time to be raised to the developing countries during the industrialization period. Then, the long time working time brought to the developing countries' workers to it is poor for labor health. Hence, although employers can raise productivity, but they need many workers to work long time to cause unhealthy. The majority found that the prediction on leisure is of the variations between world regions , due to income level exist, making European variety of capitalism. So, the First World War caused income inequality within countries and between nation states, trends in working hours , world poverty and ever growing needs (consumerism) and the like. Thus, the developed western countries' workers can work lesser time to compare to the developing Asia countries' workers. Consequently, First World War brought negative impact to influence the developing Asia countries' worker unhealthy and physical and mental illnesses number had been increasing as well as it brought positive impact to influence the labor productivity had been increasing to the Asia countries' employers, due to their workers need to work long time every day.

It seems on the positive impact hand, that the First World War caused the inflation occurrence to bring more money supply and gold supply to be raised to influence global economic growth. But, on the negative impact hand, it also brought low working hours in European developed countries and high working hours to the Asia developing countries which are needed to do different occupations in developing countries as well as the income inequality caused unfair social challenge had also occurred in developed countries, such as Europe, UK, US etc. and developing countries, such as China, Japan, Korea etc . Thus, First World War had brought developed countries better economy development and better salary and less working hours to labors because Europe had reached the mature stage of industrialization to avoid labors who needed to work overtime. Otherwise, it had brought developing countries poor economy development and poor salary and labors need work long time to raise productivities.

In conclusion, it implied that the First World War had bought some bad influences to developing countries' economic system, e.g. social income inequality, working hours inequality, inflation and GDP per capita going down in the past Europe economic history development, but it also bought welfares to developed countries' European labor working time intellectual mood to change labor productivity, it would be a 15-18 hours working week for more enlightened leisure to Europe labors. So, it seemed to cause negative economic influence to developing countries, but it cause positive economic influence to developed counties during the First World War time.

CHAPTER SEVEN

How underground train MTR can let passengers to feel catching time reducing to raise fare competitive effort

It has close relationship between globalization and global tranport development. How globalisation impacts on the environment via changes taking place in the transport sectors. In fact, it is not clear how the relative price changes that result from openness will affect the environental composition of economic activity. For example, some countries will produce more environmentally intensive goods, others will produce fewer. On the other hand, liberalisation will raise incomes, perhaps increasing the willingness to pay for environmental improvement. These potential income effects increased outweigh the negative scale effects with increased economic activities. When combined with the positive effects with technology transfer, the net effect on local pollutants could be positive . Hence, we need to find methods to solve the problem of raising transport economic activities and serious environmental pollution creating as the same time occurrence.

Globalisation helps to facilitate greater division of labor, and to exploit its comparative advantage more completely. In longer term, globalization also stimilates technology an dlabour transfers, and allows the dynamism that accompanies economic activities to stimulate the development of new transport technologies and short time transport processes that lead to global welfare improvement.

On shipping transport industry aspect, shipping will increase ocean pollution, when international shipping activities are increasing. Trade and shipping encourages energy use in shipping is coupled with the movement of waterborne commerce. The estimates depending on the transport goods number of at-sea or in port days much increase globally every day. The energy demand of international shipping fuel sale number and domestically assigned fuel sales number also increases for global fuel usage. Estimates of ocean going ships now consume about 2% to 3% and perhaps even as much as 4% of world fossil fuels.Hence, when global shipping energy fuel usage number increases, because global shipping trading activities number increases. It will bring the environmental pollution to ocean level increases.

On air transport industry aspect, their travellers‘ catching air plans travelling needs and businesses' goods transport air delivery service needs are increasing from the requirements for high quality , fast and reliable international transport. Moreover, the networks that airline companies operate have changed often to hub-and spoke networks, many new often low -cost companies have entered the air freight market, any long time air journey is needed, e.g. Australia airline expands its one new air journey flies to UK, it needs two days flying time. It means that every flight to UK from Australia , it needs to use more fuel to fly. Then , air pollution will increase also.

On road transport industry aspect, global road transport cost and transit times, traffic jam occurrence chances also increase because when the road building number is increasing globally. So, it will cause traffic jam and long journey time spending , even fuel usage spending number is also increased. Then, accident occurrence chance is raised. Hence, global business or entertainment transport activities number increasing , it will bring much negative impact on environmental pollution, traffic jams number increases, long journey spending time increases, fuel usage number increases. Although , frequent transport activities may bring GDP income.

On transport service industy aspect, but is also brings negative influence to standard of living. It means that when transport fuel demand increases, transport activities number increases, GDP income on relative any transport activities needs industy , e.g. logistic demand needs, when lorry drivers need to drive lorries to deliver goods from one warehouse to another warehouse or supermarket or office etc. different business places on the road driving activities increase. But, it also bring air pollution , traffic noise and traffic jam etc. transport problems to road and natural environment and raises worse standard of living , bad emotion to working people or learning emotion to students , due to frequent traffic jam causes , low efficiency and productivity to workers, even student individual learning time can be reduced if they need to spend long time to wait bus, ferry, rail, underground train to go to schools , due to frequent long time traffic jam occurs on the roads to influence they can not go to schools on time often when they are catching buses to go to schools absolutely in busy transport time.

Thus, although any countries need to consider how to design their transport system, e.g. how to e.g. how to choose the right locations to build roads to let many cars can be driven available easily when the morning and evening (office and school transport busy time, e.g. 6:00 to 9:00 AM morning, 6:00 to 9:00 PM in the evening transport time usually because these two transport periods are usually , there are many students and working people need to catch any public transportation or drive cars tools to go back homes. So, enough roads number and long and not narrow road area must be needed to design in order to let enough cars be driven on the roads in the transport busy times to the countries have many big cities or have high population , such as UK, US, China, India, Hong Kong. They have many people , but drivers and cars numbers both are increasing. So, efficient road design and road number are also needed to increase in order to let drivers can transport goods to deliver, students and working people can catch any public transport tools to arrive any destinations on reads in the short time rapidly in order to avoid to spend long time transportation time and late to arrive any destinations in possible occurrence. So, any sudden traffic jam is not hoped to be caused by easy traffic accidents occurrence any time.

Hence, global efficient road transport system is needed, when global transport activities are increased, because any road logistic transport activities are increasing, they will also influence the students and working people when they also need to catch any public transport tools or drive themselves cars to go to working places or schools on the roads at the same busy transport time between 6:00 to 9:00 AM morning busy transport time and between 6:00 to 9:00 PM evening busy transport time. Because these both times will be have many students, working people , they need either go to offices or schools or go to homes. Hence, if the country had many lorry drivers need to drive their lorries to deliver goods on the roads in the transport busy morning or evening time in the same driving time on the roads. It will increase the risk to cause frequent traffic jam or traffic accident occurrence easily in possible in the country. So, any countries' governments can not neglect how to design roads and choose anywhere are the roads suitable locations to be built as well as anywhere land useful number to build road location choices in order to solve geographical traffic jams occurrence chance.

Hence, globalization of transport activities may bring geographical GDP growth, but it also bring traffic jams and traffic accidents occurrences, hearing impairment due to traffic noise, air pollution, traffic crashed, bad working emotions to workers and bad learning emotions to students, due to spending long transport time when traffic jam or traffic accidence occurs more easily.

However, transportation is an important tool if a country's progress. Rapid economic growth and increasing level of urbanization enhances a person's living standard have, it leads to a greater travel demands. Hence, governments ought not neglect have to design its roads , measure every road's length or width whether it has how many cars need to drive in morning or evening transport busy time for students, working people and delivery goods drivers of public transportation tools or private transportation tools easy driving needs in order to avoid frequent traffic jams or traffic accidents occurrences in possible.

Moreover, any governments also need to solve these issues, if they hope to develop their transport system successfully. These issues include : What mode of transportation to cost-effective in meeting a region's transportation needs to the country? How should a state department of transportation prioritize its highway delivers to maximize economic growth? What is the trade-off between additional growth in urban area and the cost of expanding transportation systems to accommodate greater growth? What effect does the expansion of transportation systems have on the need to invest in other types of transport modes? For example , the transport expansion may include the construction of additional highway segments, rail lines, runways, or additional sea, air, rail or bus terminal capacity using traditional technology; highway may include the additional of lanes to an interstate highway system; the conversion of an existing two-lane road to a four lane limited access highway, replacement or widening of bridges, and the extension of an existing road. Airport examples, include runway lengthening, apron expansion, and additional terminal gates.

On the other hand, enhancement to new transport technologies may bring efficiency of the existing highway system, examples may include intelligent highway systems, congestion pricing, intermodal freight facilities, geographic positioning systems, and instrument landing systems to mention of a few major transport innovations. So, transport policy makers need to understand the effects of these new transport mode innovations on economic development or GDP growth on transport activities growth transportation services and a more efficient use of limited land supplying scarce resources , air quality ,and noise pollution, traffic jams, long spending transport time to students, working people, entertaining people, even deliver goods lorry drivers their every day essential driving activities or catching public transportation tools needs problems. For example, the concept of intelligent highway systems needs increase trend. In simply , vehicles are being linked to each other and to traffic control devices to improve the efficiency of the total highway system. Similar types of innovations in intelligent traffic management are increasing needs for air, sea, and rail systems. The question is that whether intelligent highway systems can attribute of highways on economic development, raising on productivity of reducing highway congestion or improving pavement condition.

In fact, many developed countries' transportation system is mature. The nation has gone beyond the frontier of building, the interstate highway system and connecting most cities (markets). Tweaking the system with additional lanes and the new intelligent highway systems are useful in China, US, UK, because they have many cities. SO, road efficient traffic congestion control is needed when many students, working people, delivery goods transport people need to drive cars or catch cars on every city's roads in the transport busy time between 6:00 to 9:00 AM morning transport busy time as well as between 6:00 to 9:00 PM evening transport busy time.

However, transportation investment must be needed, if the country hoped to have good economic productivity, efficient transport service can bring good effects on the flows goods and people on roads every day when they use the country's transport system. So, any countries need to collect data, they can not be lack of enough transport information in any time that links anywhere locations of any drivers to the locations of the transport system that provide them with services in any time, e.g. every day morning and evening transport busy time, radio can report the real transport time of any roads traffic jam or traffic accident message to let drivers to listen to know whether anywhere roads are occurring traffic accidents or traffic jams or when the road traffic accident or traffic jam is solved to let the drivers can know whether when the roads can be opened to drive again. So, real time road transport message information is needed to report by radio, in order to let any drivers to know whether they ought choose to drive themselves cars on the road when they need to choose anywhere road to drive to the destination if they can know when the road has traffic accident or traffic jam occurs. They won't drive their cars on the road in the moment immediately.

On conclusion, globalization can being frequent transport economic activities. So, road , air, sea, transport service users' transport service needs are also increased. Every country ought not neglect how to innovate their transport service in order to satisfy their transport needs to achieve economic growth, efficient and short transport time spending, productivities increase, reducing air pollution, traffic noise , raisins standard of living on transport influence aspect to satisfy working people, students, entertaining people, delivery goods transport users' efficient road transport time behavioral spending aspect.

On conclusion, when one country's electric public transport tool service increases, it may cause gas need decreases and gas business will experience decline stage cycle stage rapidly.

CHAPTER EIGHT

How immigration and climate change influences general social sale increases

How immigration influences the country demand increases and general social sale price increases when the country's people number is increasing?

What are immigration impacts to social econoomy? Immigration how influences into a region impacts house prices in three ways. For a fixed level of local population, housing demand rises due to the increase in foreign-born population. In addition, immigrants can influence native location decisions and induce additional shifts in house demand.

Does immigration cause housing prices to be higher ? In applied economic view, economists determined that illigration contributed to no more than 0.1% to 0.12% increase in housing prices. Furthermore, an increase in new housing construction in response to higher demand also moderated the effect of immigration.

What impact did immigration have on society? The available evidence suggests that immigration leads to more innovation, in better educated workforce, greater occupational specialization, better working of skills with jobs, and higher overall economic productivity. Immigration also has a not positive effect on combined local budgets.

How does overpopulation affect housing by increasing immigrant number? Population change leads to a changing demand for housing population growth, and particularly the growth in the number of housing population growth, and particularly the growth in the number of households leads to a growth in hosing demand. Population decline might in the long term, leads to a decrease in housing demand.

However, immigration also brings good aspect to economy, instead of netagive aspect. The available evidence suggests that immigration leads to more innovation, a better educated workforce, greater occupational specialization, better matching of skills with jobs, and higher overall economic productivity. Immigration boosts the well-being of the society. If the growth rate of per-capita income increases thanks to immigrants, the standard of living of the general population can rise. For canada exampls, immigration can bring positive impact to Canada's economy. The 2026 census found that immigrants had median earnings of $29,770 compared to $36,300 for native born Canadians. Recent immigrants are far more likely than native born canadians to initially have low incomes, with income and employment rates increasing towards the national average with more than spent in canada.

What are the positive or negative impact to immigration? The channels have both positive and negative static and dynamic effects. One netagive static effect of immigration is that migration directly reduces the available supply of labour, particularly skilled labour, but these are positive static effects , such as through return migration and remittances.

The positive impacts of migration may include the opportunity to get a better job, improved quality of life, safety from conflict. The opportunity of a better education. The negative impacts of migration may include: Poverty makes them unable to live a normal and healthy life. Children growing up in pvoerty have no access to proper nutrition, education or health. Migration increased the slum areas in cities which increase many problems, such as unhygienic conditions, crime, pollution etc.

How does migration affect the economy in global? The available evidence suggests that immigration leads to more innovation, a better educated workforce, greater occupational specialization, better matching of skills with jobs, and higher overall economic productivity. Moreover, immigration also have has a not positive effect on improving productivity to the country's manufacturers aspect, for example, labour migrants have the most positive impacts on either positive or negative terms. The impact is negative, it brings small impact of the human capital brought by migrants on skillful manufacturing jobs aspect. As the same time, emigration can have a positive impact on development. Positive impacts on host countries, reducing job vacancies number and improving skills by overseas skillful immigrants. Also, returning migrants can bring savings, skills and international contacts.

Hence, the economic effects of migration, it indicates that high skilled migrants bring diverse talent and expertise, when foolish or poor skillful workers are improved or upgrade high skill and has no negative efffects on public fiances as immigration is found to have an overall positive impact on economic growth in long term. Moreover, the positive impact not just on population growth. Many migrants bring higher education and skill. The expanded attributed allow the modeling to better capture both the positive and negative impacts.

On conclusion, migrants have positive impact on developing countries called " how immigrants contribute to developing countries economies, e.g. leading a greater cultural diversity, social benefits, raising economic costs to manufacturers, e.g. reducing manufacturing cost, assisting refugees , e.g. households wealth, increasing due to they can find jobs to do easily when they emmigrate to the another country, such as migrant workers are an aset to the country where they bring their knowledge and skill to attribute to the new country's society. Hence, I think that immigration can bring many advantages to a country both for the economy and society as a whole.

Does health reason influence developing countries people to choose migration by climate change impact?

Climate change is caused substantial increases in population movement. It has considered the likely causal influences much movement and the risks to national and international security. But, there has been little research on the consequences of climate-related migration and the health of people who move. May health impacts of climate change play important role in population movement?

However, climate change-related migration is likely to result in adverse health outcomes, particularly in situations of forced migration. In fact, climate change is widely projected to cause substantial increases in the scale of human population movement. Forecasts of the number of people who will move by around midcentury in response to the effects of climate change vary from tens of millions to 250 million people (United Nations High Commissions For Refugees (UNHCR, 2009).

Many scientists believe migration reason is common that the countries' people are fear of diseases and climate change environmental disasters to be caused in their countries, especially developing countries by climate change negative influences. Specially, populations in low-income countries whose health is most at risk from climate changes and where. There are often high pre-existing levels of health problems are used to coping with adverse health outcomes without causing to migration. So, it is likely that population movement that is driven substantially by health risks will occur only where those risks are sufficiently serious and widespread. For example, Africa the country's climate change will bring the risk of infectious disease (e.g. cholera , measles, malaria, meningitis) to Africa. In fact, Africa has adequate health care systems, low immunization coverage, lack of clean water and poor sanitation (Zarocostas, 2011).

Thus, it seems that climate change will bring health rick challenge to the country to influence people to choose to migrate other countries. Although, the range and extent of health risks with future climate related population movements can't be clearly forever, but the evidence of health outcomes of movement of people indicates that health risks will predominate over health benefits. This often is an issue of considerable geopolitical, ethical and economic importance. Consequently, it has close cause and effect relationship between climate change and health risk to cause people to choose migration.

Impact of population growth and population ethics on climate change mitigation

Future population growth migration number is uncertain, due to climate change factor influence. Higher mitigation growth entails more emissions and means either more people will choose to mitigate other better climate countries to live or the better climate countries will have more people to immigrate to live, due to any sudden climate change environment related impacts.

However, some climate scientists feel how future population is related importantly determines mitigation decisions. They indicated that some bad climate countries' people make any mitigation decision choice, it responds to the fact that a larger population means climate change hurts more people. For example, in 2025 year assuming United Nations has high rather than low population scenario entails an increase in the social cost of carbon dioxide (SCC) of 85% under total utilitarianism (TU), vs 5% under average utilitarianism (AU). The difference is the (SCC) between the two population scenarios under (TU) is comparable to commonly debated decisions regarding time discounting. Additionally, they estimate the avoided mitigation costs implied by reductions in population growth, finding that large neat term savings US $6billions amount annually occur under (TU).

Hence, it seems that climate changing is one important factor to bring any bad climate change countries which need to pay large disaster expenditure to recover their economy after any sudden serious climate change impacts.

How climate change impacts on food price rises ?

In fact, climate change will increase global temperature change rainfall patterns and will result in more frequent and severe floods and drought. Depending on future emission of greenhouse gases, global temperatures are likely to rise between 2 degree and 4 degree within the next century. The main impacts of climate change will however not be felt through higher temperatures, but through a change in the hydrological cycle. Rainfall is likely to increase around the poles and the tropics when in the sub-tropics average precipitation is likely to decrease. Not only the average annual or seasonal rainfall will change, there also be an increase in the number of extreme events resulting in most frequent and severe floods and droughts.

How does climate change influence to development countries? Climate change will influence any development countries on these several aspects. They include as below:

On trade influence hand, reducing emission levels from the developing world is extremely important. If current developments are continuing, for example, emissions from China and India both countries will save be much higher than the total emission form all Europe countries. Currently, the Europe is stimulating mitigation and transfer of clean technologies through the clean development mechanism (CDM). Although, it is still unclear what the mitigation potential of the (CDM) is, especially in India the investment is (CDM) projects is significant. However, the Europe should take a much wider approach. In developing countries a lot can be done in terms of increasing energy efficiency, land use change and agriculture. It is also important that developing countries are stimulated to choose a sustainable, low emission developed pathway. Choices for more sustainable, low emission technologies should be made early in the process. It seems that climate changing will encourage many countries will choose to do more environment protection related trading, e.g. researching how to invent environment protection new products to reduce our earth pollution between European and any developing countries, such as China and India etc.

On focus mitigation efforts in least developed countries on land use change, agriculture development aspect, in the least developed countries mitigation efforts should not focus on the energy or transport sector, but on agriculture and forestry. Agriculture is responsible for a relatively large percentage of the emissions in many developing countries, e.g. Africa, China, Malaysia, Hong Kong, Japan etc. In this sector there are many win options both reducing poverty and reducing greenhouse gas emissions. For example, improved water and nutrient management can sharply increase production efficiency and reduces at least the amount of emission per kg food produced. Agro-forestry reduces greenhouse gas emission through increased carbon storage and reduces poverty through diversifying the incomes of local communities.

However, in most developing countries, the main limitation in coping with the impacts of climate change is a lack of capacity. Besides a lack of capacity, in many developing countries, there is also a significant lack of data and knowledge on climate change impacts. Developing countries should be stimulated to improve data gathering and make existing data more easily available.However, no migration effort will stop the need for adaptation. Especially, the least developed countries, who have contributed little to the problem will suffer the most.

On business strategies for climate change aspect, nowadays, the valuation for clean-technology companies, have increased considerable and the corporate carbon footprint has become an important topic to be discussed how to solve among senior managers? How can firms profit from what they do to address climate change? Thus, a low-carbon economy is already especially in energy, transport and heavy industry.

If current climate science holds true and there is considerable uncertainty in the estimates, global greenhouse gas emissions should ideally decrease from today's levels by 90 percent as of 2050 year in order to certain global warming below two degrees centigrade. Hence, it seems global warmth challenge brings further any new energy potential development businesses. Due to environment scientists encourage us to be realized the necessary increase in carbon productivity and new low-carbon technologies that are necessary dramatically reduces energy consumption and direct greenhouse gas emissions will have to be developed and then implemented widely to avoid future serious global environment warmth caused climate changes and pollution challenges occurrence.

What are the cause and effect economy relationship between climate change and environment migration to influence food sale price changes?

The choice of migration reasons can include that seeking better job chance, better job environment, better salary, better standard of life, better education, less crimes, feeling more safety etc. different psychological reasons. However, whether climate changing will be one factor to cause migration. This is one psychological life adaption issue. Some people may accept to adapt to live worse life when their countries are encountering any natural environment or economic negative or climate negative change or social negative impact suddenly. Otherwise, some people may not accept to adapt to live worse life when they countries are encountering any worse influences suddenly, such as sudden worse climate change. Thus, to research that whether it has relationship to influence migration choice between climate change and migration. We need to know whether what the general acceptable level to adapt climate change to human is.

It means that if the climate change has exceeded the countries' general people's acceptable level to adapt to live in their countries. Then, it is possible that it will cause many people do not feel more adaptive to live in their countries forever, due to serious sudden climate change disaster occurrence.

What is the general acceptable level to live to their countries to adaptive climate change? However, before they choose to migrate, they will mind these questions usually. How can they migrate? Once they leave, who will guard their land? How will they support their family in the city?

Environment problems are both sudden and gradual have always causal different formed of displacement around the world, but recent studied have emphasized that more people are likely to migrate in the future, owing to climate change (Stern, N. 2007).

In fact, climate change will bring serious challenge to any countries, such as natural resources shortage, lacking more productive livelihoods supply. Then, it views this question: If migration have no adaptive potential, then what can be done (or is being done) to facilitate communities to migrate? Analyzing

who migrants, how, why and where they go can provide useful insights for development planners aiming to support poor families. It seems that every family member's adaptive to live factor will influence the whole family who decides to choose to migrate or stay in their country when climate change disaster sudden occurs.

However, environmental migration is typically internal and short term, the potential for conflict is that unstable urban and rural demographics are related to higher risks of civil war and low level conflicts to environment migration during periods of environmental stress are common. Also, I believe that the impact of climate change can be divided into two distinct drivers of migration:

Climate processes driver , such as sea-level rise, shortage of agricultural land, desertification and growing water scarcity and climate events , such as flooding, storms. But, non-climate drivers, such as government policy, population growth and community level resilience to natural disaster are also important. All contribute to the degree of people's adaptive level.

The climate change problem is one of time (the speed of change) and scale (the number of people it will affect). Although, temporary migration is as an adaptive response to climate stress is already apparent in many areas. But the ability to migrate is a function of mobility and resources (both financial and social). IN other words, the people most to climate change are not necessary the one's most likely to migrate among of different migration factors.

In fact, predicting future flows of climate migrants is complex. Professor Myers' estimate of 200 million climate migrants by 2050 year has become the accepted figure-cities in respected publications from the IPCC to the Stern Review on the economics of climate change (Stern, N., Ed. 2006).Hence, it seems that there will have many different factors to cause climate migrant number rising in the future.

Consequently, migration and resettlement may be the most threatening short-term effects of climate change on human settlements. People may decide to migrate in any of the following cases. They includes: loss of housing (because of river, or sea flooding or mudslides), loss of living resources (like water, energy and food supply or employment affected by climate changes); loss of social and cultural resources (loss of cultural properties, neighborhood or community networks).

The three main climate change impacts to influence people to live may include that sea level rise: rising average sea level, sale water intrusion in aquifers, water availability (increase/decrease), extreme weather event: drought, heat waves, violent storms, floods. Thus, if any one of these environment change factors impacts to influence general people's life adaptive level to live anywhere in their any geographic location of their countries. Then, it is possible to influence them to choose to be environmental migrants. It means persons or group of persons who, for compelling reasons of sudden or progressive changes in the environment that adversely affect their lives or living conditions are obliged to leave their habitual homes, or choose to do so, either temporarily or permanently and who move either within their country or abroad. Thus, climate change can let them to feel that it is one unsafe natural disaster and it only brings negative effect to them when they still choose to live in their home town. It refers to situations where people are displaced across boarders in the context of sudden or slow onset disasters or in the context of the adverse effects of climate change.

In forces to non-forces mobility psychological view point, environmental refugee will have these three stages to decide migration: First stage is , refugee –like situation stage, it is very low level control over the whole process , vulnerability. Second stage is, environmentally driven displacement stage, it is compelled, but voluntary, more control over timing and direction and less vulnerability than refugees, but less control and more vulnerability than migrants. Final stage is migrant like situations stage, it is greater control over the process and less vulnerability , even if people are moving in response to deteriorating conditions (Hugo, G. 1996).

Consequently, climate change will be one main important factor to cause any country people who choose to do environmental migrants decision to compare other factors. IT seems, that climate change factor and environment migrant which have close relationship to cause any country people who choose to migrate more than social , economy , less crime, education, cultural , job change, standard of life etc. different external non-natural environment factors.

Climate change how influences global energy need ?

We are facing global warmth and natural resource and energy shortage challenges. Due to our Earth have limited natural resource numbers to supply to us to manufacture energy, but global population has been increasing every year. Thus, it is possible that we have energy shortage crisis. Also, manufactures are spending too much energy to waste to manufacture any products, the energy will cause air or water pollution in manufacturing process or drivers are driving their vehicles to pollute air on the roads. Then it will cause global warmth crisis. How we can avoid these both crises to occur. I shall give some recommendation as below:

Primary energy exploration method

- Greenhouse primary gas energy

Have you ever seen a greenhouse? A greenhouse can trap heat in the sunlight and keeps the air inside the greenhouse warm enough for plants to grow. The glass roof and walls of a greenhouse let in sunlight but prevent heat from escape, this makes the greenhouse warm inside. Similarly, some gases in the Earth's atmosphere can trap heat from the sun and keep the Earth warm. This is called the greenhouse effect. The gases energy that can trap heat from the sun are called greenhouse gases. It is future one kind of potential primary energy to reduce environmental pollution new energy products for human consuming.

- Underwater primary water energy

The world's underwater meeting took place around a table about five meters underwater. Many scientists believe that due to melting of ice caused by global warming, the sea level will rise by as much as 1 m by the end of this century. If the level of the sea rises in the future, most regions of the country will be underwater.

What impact of global warming is mentioned by underground water?
Can human apply underwater water technology to explore natural underground water energy to avoid global warming threat?

Why do we need to Safety in using fuel and handle gas leaks? Why do we feel town gas smell? How is electricity located at electric station far away from town area? How to solve problems caused by the use of fossil fuels? How to reduce the use of fossil fuels?

To solve the problems, the best way is to reduce our used of fossil fuel. This helps prevent fossil fuels form being used up too quickly. Also, it helps us to reduce environmental problems because fewer pollutants are given out when less fossil fuels are used. Can human help to reduce the use of fossil fuels? Fossil fuels are mainly in power station. Although we use some fossil fuels for our gas cooker and car, it won't make much difference if I use less.

Fossil fuel is not used renew primary energy. Most of energy we use come from fossil fuels, for example, the electricity we use is generated in power stations by burning fossil fuels. The buses we ride use diesel oil.

Therefore, we can help reduce the use of fossil fuels by saving energy in our daily lives.

The actions that we can take such as: setting the air-conditioner to a higher temperature, walking instead of using lift, taking a short shower instead of a bath. This reduces the use of the hot water and thus the energy needed to heat the water. Thus, many people can help a lot to reduce our use of fossil fuels to avoid fossil fuel shortage risk occurrence.

For Hong Kong people energy consumption case, how much energy is used when a person travels from Hong Kong to Beijing by airplane? (The distance between Hong Kong and Beijing is about 2000 km). How much energy is used when Hong Kong people take a bus form Tai PO city to Central city? How much energy is used if Hong Kong people drive a car instead? (The driving distance between Tai Po city and Central city is 10Km).

Science explorer, we can visit the England website. Find ways to reduce energy usage from UK people energy using methods. Energy is very important to us. We need energy to walk and carry on any actions. We need energy to grow. We also need energy from food to survive. Without energy, we will die. All machines we use need energy. Without energy the electrical appliances in our homes won't work, the machines in factories will stop.

There are different forms of energy, e.g. light, heat, sound, wind, water, electrical kinetic, chemical and potential energy. Some form energy is primary energy and it can not renew to use, e.g. light, sound, wind, water, fossil fuel etc. Some form energy is secondary energy and it can renew to use in possible, e.g. nuclear, electric charge battery etc. Why does human need to concern how to manufacture secondary energy? Because it is possible that our natural resource will be consumed all, thus we will face primary energy shortage risk. If human can invent any new form of man-made secondary energy to renew to use in order to avoid primary energy shortage to supply to use to use, then human won't only depend on our Earth natural resource energy supply numbers. We can invent any new secondary energy to renew to use again either replaces primary energy or instead of primary energy limit number supply.

What is energy change? For television energy change power case. Firstly, electrical energy changes to television power to be used by television itself, then it changes to light power, next it changes to light power. How to choose fuel form to use? Due to energy can change to different form of powers to supply different form of power advantages to supply to human to use, so it is possible that we can also invent any secondary man made renew used energy to change different form powers to supply us to use, e.g. nuclear energy changes to light or sound or heat form of powers ; electrical charge batteries changes to light or sound or heat form powers to satisfy our daily life needs.

For primary natural resource fuel energy example, different fuel has different feature, e.g. easy to burn, safe to use, gives out a lot of energy, inexpensive, produces little air pollution, easy to transport and store. How can we use in different channels, such as heating food, hot pat, driving vehicles.

For example, although coal is not expensive to cause electricity energy for past transportation tool, e.g. traditional coal energy train or our daily home cooking, but it has negative influence to environment air pollution. Hence, we ought to follow the primary natural resource energy's feature to decide how to apply what aspects of our life needs.

For example, if the country's people hope to reduce pollution when who use any kind of energy, e.g. US , Europe energy markets. The energy entrepreneur ought concentrate on manufacturing the kind of energy which can reduce environment pollution to be the least level to supply the country people to use, e.g. electric charge battery supplies to these countries' drivers to drive their vehicles on the roads, wind energy or water energy to manufacture electricity power supply to reduce air or water pollution ; or if the country people hope to buy the inexpensive energy to use, even the energy's quality and performance is worse, e.g. China, India, Hong Kong markets. The energy entrepreneur ought concentrate on manufacturing the lowest cost and enough supply of natural resource to manufacture the kind of energy to sell cheap price to these countries to use, e.g. China, Africa can accept to use e.g. gas, coal, fuel energy to use to compare developed countries people, e.g. UK, US; or if the countries people who hope to use energy which can easy to transport and store, e.g. light coal. The energy entrepreneur can choose to concentrate on manufacturing much coal to supply to the countries people to use, e.g. China, Arica Thus, to choose to manufacture which kinds of energy supply to the countries market people to use, the energy entrepreneur how decides to manufacture which kind of energy, it depends on which kinds of fuel advantages of the countries people most concerning.

How climate change raises secondary energy need and sale price increase ?

Secondary energy commercial worth

What is energy meaning? It is defined a dynamic quality, it is a fundamental entity of nature that is transferred between parts of a system in the production of physical change within the system, and it is usually regarded as the capacity for doing work, and it is usable power (such as heat or electricity) or the resources for producing such power.

Why does secondary energy own investment worth? Because the different forms of primary natural resource energy will have supply shortage crisis, such as natural resources coal, gas, solar, wind, water, geothermal, biomass(organic material) etc. However, human can attempt to explore any undiscovered Earth or Space resource to manufacture any kinds of secondary energies, e.g. nuclear energy, electric recharge battery energy to supply to electric vehicle or space robots transportation tools to use or satisfy our daily life needs in future one day. So any kind of undiscovered secondary man-made renewed used energy resources have potential commercial worth to any energy entrepreneurs, it is possible that they can replace traditional primary energy to supply to human to use for our different aspects of life needs. In the future, the secondary energy demand will increase, when primary energy supply number has decreased form natural exploration. So, it will cause the effect of any demand of secondary energy product to be raised and prices to be increased in possible. Due to global population has been growing up, considerably China and India both countries populations have been increasing rapidly. Scientists predict there are more than 1.2 billion people worldwide will lack access to electricity, and more than 2.5 billion still use wood, charcoal to cook and heat in the future when primary energy has no enough number to supply to us to use. Hence, the fact that demand is this much greater than supply to make energy a prime market for further growth.

● Energy investment risks

Although, secondary energy will have much investment worth, but energy like all other investments will carry risks. The internal and external risk factors include such as: policy is always changing to prohibit which do energy trading more easily between the energy exporting and importing countries, the secondary energy manufacturer itself own abilities to invent and to manufacture any kinds of secondary energy, improved technology can quickly make an technology obsolete, geopolitical rifts can happen overnight, the country's energy consumer (user)'s preferable choice to use which either kinds of secondary energy or secondary energy. So, it seems that (man-made) renewed used secondary energy industry can provide above-average returns, but it can also bring high risk commercial investment.

- Ways to solve energy exploration challenge

Traditionally, energy supply companies will apply those methods to operate energy providing businesses. For Shell,. Exxon examples, which had own gas stations, explore and drill for gas on their own. Other companies specialize in a part of the energy market, e.g. leasing oil rigs for example, or operating a pipeline. Energy supplying companies can choose to manufacture any kinds of energy to supply, e.g. trade oil, gas, coal, uranium, electricity etc. Any energy price and supply is demanded on the countries energy users' which kinds of energy most choice need or certain energy commodities to be chose to use popularly. For example, if US most people prefer to use secondary man-made renew used energy more than primary energy. Then, US energy manufacturers ought concentrate on manufacturing much different kinds of secondary man-made renew used energy to prepare to supply to its domestic US market in order to raise secondary energy price to sell in its country. So, the energy manufacturer's energy manufacturing choice, it is depend on which the country's people prefer to use which kinds of energy for their daily life needs.

However, scientists predict secondary energy market will have large market share, due to primary energy will have shortage to explore to supply in our earth and future energy consumers(users) prefer to choose to use more efficiency, less energy consumption, none environment pollution cause, cost effectiveness, renew to use of any kinds of energy. For example, the electricity recharge battery secondary man-made renew used energy is one kind of reducing air pollution power to push any electric battery vehicles to be driven to compare gas energy during drivers are driving their cars on the roads. They can reduce noise and air pollution and drivers can drive safely, who only need to buy one electric recharge battery to recharge in any electric recharge battery stations on streets when the electric recharge battery has no enough power to push their cars and they need to recharge their electric recharge battery drive when they had driven between one to two days. Due to primary energy, e.g. fuel , gas, the kinds of primary energies will have shortage to supply to global drivers to drive their traditional cars. Thus, the electric recharge battery or any undiscovered secondary energy will be future driving market needs. So, man-made renew used secondary energy, e.g. biofuel, hydro-electric, nuclear, will be one kind of efficient, clean, less pollution cause, cost-effective of energy to supply to our global vehicle market, even any other undiscovered new markets. Supposing they are popular to be used for electric vehicle market globally in future one day, then their prices will be decreased and constructed to average car requires up to 1,700 gallons of oil. Also supposing that making average computer requires more than ten times or weight to fossil fuels, every calories of food eaten in the US requires roughly then calories of fossil fuels. Hence, cheap energy will be one successful factor to influence future potential energy consumer (user) individual choice needs. Conversely, ion good economic times, people are more willing to travel, to buy products, and all of which success demand and low process for energy.

- Food production secondary energy need

In the future, secondary energy will be the best choice to food production market. The modern food production system is essentially a success of changing fossil fuels into food. So, raising energy prices are almost higher food costs and even shortage for fossil fuels energy. If one day, one kind of discovered secondary man-made renew used energy can supply to any restaurants or homes to be used to cook at the cheap price, then the profit is very high for this kind of food production energy. Thus, future food production secondary energy consumption market is large and because the primary energy inputs for agriculture are higher than the energy outputs of the food. However, future secondary man-made renew used energy for food production system is only one part of whole energy consumer in food industry. The food production is related to whole food consumption market which includes: household cooking energy market, agriculture or vegetable, rice, fruit etc. foods farming machines energy market, food manufacturing factories market, food machine package market, transportation food delivery market, supermarket or fruit/food sale stores market. They must need any energy inputs to achieve the food production or food transportation or warehouse / stores electricity supply or cooking energy needs. Hence, these food suppliers relate to any whole food factory manufacturers, food retailers, food wholesalers, farmers and home/restaurant cookers, all of them must need to use energy to carry on their food producing or food cooking or food transportation activities every day in overall food industry. Thus, it seems that undiscovered any second energy demand will be increased, when the primary energy supply number is decreasing. Also, when people can accept to use secondary energy to replace primary energy to be used for any cooking, transporting food, manufacturing food, food retail stores or warehouse food delivery energy need activities. Then, the secondary energy price will be fall down to attract many food energy consumers.

Nowadays, the food industry energy may includes primary nature resource gas energy or electricity energy for house house families or restaurants cooking needs, food delivering lorry drivers driving needs usually. If future second man made renew used energy is invented successful popular to be used, e.g. hydrogen, electric recharged battery energy for electric vehicles or restaurant/home families cooking needs or food factories machine maufacturing energy needs. Then, the seconday energy will have possible to replace primary energy to be food industry energy market.

Wiley, composition services graphics indicated that global primary energy consumption had been increasing 30 billion tons from 1830 year to 510 billion tons in 2010 year as well as global population size had been increasing from 70 billion 1830 yeat to 510 billion in 2010 year. Thus, it seems that global primary energy consumption will be needed largely after 2010 year. If future global nature resource primary energy is explored full number and it had not enough energy number to supply global human to use. Then, it will being many people feel uncomfortable and inconvenient,e.g. Some countries won't have enough energy to supply transportion tools to be driven, some homes and restaurants won't have enough energy to supply to cook to eat or to provide restaurant clients to eat etc. daily activies, due to human's much activities which are needs energy supply. Thus, it seems that global primary energy comsumption will be needed largely after 2010 year.

Wiley, composition services graphics also explianed that why the primary energy consumption demand can be needed to achieve the same level to the global population size increasing in 2010 year. The graph showed these reasons why cause the same level of global population size and global primary energy consumpion demand which may include: The graph showed that after a nation is developed, its per-person energy use hegins to level off. In North Ameruca and Europe, where energy demand has remained flat, or fallen dightly, in each of the past few years. But the 1.3 billion people on those two continents are far outweighted by the 5 billion people in Asia and

Africa, e.g. Chinese and Indian. who currently have more energy need to comapre average per man to North America and Europe per man, ensuring that overall energy demand will rise for years to come.

Wiley, composition services graphics also predicted that the growth in primary energy demand. China will have 4,500 million tons in 2035 year. India will have 3,000 million tons in 2035 year. Other developing Asia will have 2,000 million tons in 2035 year. Russia will have 1,500 million tons in 2035, Middle East will have 1,300 million tons in 2035, other rest of world will have 1,000 million tons in 2035. Hence, it implied that China will be the largest primary energy need country in the future.

China will be future the primary potential energy consumer market. The primary energy includes water, coal, wind, fossil oil, gas ,solar, geothermal energy, biomass (organiz material) etc. different natural resource primary energy. Otherwise, US, UK, Europe will be secondary energy potential need market. For example, electrical recharge battery energy will be raised demand to supply to any future new design electrical charge battery vehicles in US, Europe, UK markets.

Due to US, Europe, UK people concern environment protection, so they will invent many electric charge battery vehicles to consume electrical charge battery to replace polluted gas energy to avoid air pollution when the drivers are driving cars on themselve countries' roads. For example, second man-made renew used nuclear energy can be applied to rockets to pusch them to leave our earth to fly to other space far away and consuming nuclear energy will be cost efficient, and nuclear energy saving will be more when nuclear to spend long time to be used in any long time space journey. Hence, nuclear energy and electric charge battery secondary energy will be popular to be applied to vehicles and rockets energy needs in US, Europe, potential marketss, even our daily energy needs in global second energy market.

- Law and policies in engery supply industry

Every energy entrepreneur needs to consider how whose government implement law and policies to prohibit whose energy consumption, energy distribution and energy production behavior in order to protect energy consumers can have fair price energy purchase from the country's energy suppliers between themselves. For US energy law and policy example, the energy independence and security Act of 2007 year. It's major provisions include: Accelerated research of clean energy technologies Act, energy savings in building and industry Act, improved standards for appliances and lighting Act, improved vehical fuel economy Act and increased production of biofuel Act. It aims to prohibit any US energy manufacturing suppliers do any unfair energy trading transaction behavior to its domestic or foreign energy consumers immortally.

- Energy entrepreneur's business strategy

Before you decide to operate either any kinds of secondary energy or primary energy supply business or both kinds of energy supply business. I recommend that you need to consider how to solve these questions before choosing which kind of energy product to manufacture. The questions may include as below:

Who are your energy business's competitors (peers)? How do they compare? How have your energy business company performed cyclically? How to choose to manufacture to sell which kinds of primary or secondary energy product(s), either manufactures only primary energy product(s) or manufactures only secondary energy products or both? Which countries do you plan to sell your energy product?

Illustration by Wilsey, composition services graphiss showed that these natural resources to energy product the world's electricity percentage, such as below:

41% of coal, 5% of oil, 21% of gas, 13% of nuclear, 16% of Hydro, 3% other renewable secondary man-made energy.

Hence, coal will be future the major natural resource to produce electricity. The energy entrepreneur ought attempt to explore any coal resources, when who choose to supply electricity power to consumers for future energy consumption country markets.

Wiley, composition services also predicted that the expectation is that North America coal will supply the expectation is that North America coal will supply Asian demand, Us export terminals have a total capacity of 173 million tommes output. China will drive 16% of the nations total output. China will drive the sea-born demand for coal over for the forcessable future. Chinese energy consumption will grow more than 12 % between 1980 and 2009 years. Though, China heads global demand, India is growing faster in terms of coal imports. Much of the global coal demand will be supplied by Indonesia and Australia. Colombia, Russia, South Africa and Mongolia are also players in global export coal energy resources.

Consequently, I believe that secondary energy will be one kind of new energy product to replace traditional primary energy product for human energy consumption market global needs. Hence, it is right time any energy entrepreneur needs to research how to explore any undiscovered man-made renew used secondary energy products to avoid primary energy shortage crisis occurrence.

How climate change influences migrant decision to bring economy influence ?

How and why climate change influence migrant right change ? When migrant right change, how it influence migrant immigrating desire ? The interlinkages between climate change and human rights are deep and complex, with climate change impacting a wide range of internationally protected human rights; such as rights to health and even life and rights to food, water, shelter and property. In this paper, I am going to discuss the effect of climate change on protected human rights relating to migration, focusing primarily on the relationship between international refugee law and climate change.

There remains uncertainty on how severe global warming will be and its precise impacts on society, but there is a 97 per cent consensus among experts that a rapid build-up of greenhouse gas is due to human activities.The Earth's climate is gradually changing due to the continuous concentration of anthropogenic greenhouse gas (GHG) emissions into the atmosphere. The Earth's surface temperature is getting warmer at a disturbing rate, and has become significantly warmer in the last 150 years after 10,000 years of relative stability.[3] Most climate change projections are based on a two-degree Celsius increase in global mean temperature from the temperature in 1850, which has now been agreed by most States as the threshold for 'dangerous' climate change.

The consequences of climate change are more obvious now due to the increased prevalence of rising sea levels, extreme weather conditions, drought and desertification, and these consequences will have significant effects on the ecosystem, specifically on food security, migration, and health. The political, economic, and social capacity of a country, which includes its infrastructure, economic stability, and ability to help its population when in need, will affect individual's ability to cope with the impacts of climate change, and therefore the impacts will be felt differently in different communities. In the 1980s and 1990s, climate change was primarily viewed as an environmental and scientific issue, but in 1990 the potential impacts of climate change on human migration were identified by the Intergovernmental Panel on Climate Change (IPCC). The IPCC stated that millions of people would likely be uprooted by shoreline erosion, coastal flooding, and agricultural disturbances (such as salination of crops),and that climate change might require consideration of 'migration and resettlement outside of national boundaries.

However, the relationship between climate change and forced migration has emerged as one of the most studied, but contested, fields of inquiry, and the lack of agreement on the links between climate change and forced migration explains why the call for the recognition of so-called 'climate change refugees' has been unsuccessful. Legally, there is no such thing as a 'climate change refugee,' and this point will be expanded upon later in this paper, but there is, however, evidence that people are moving in response to the effects of climate change. Cross-border displacement resulting from natural disasters and the effects of climate change has therefore been identified as a normative gap in the international legal protection regime.Determining how exactly climate change affects people's decisions to move is crucial in determining how appropriate the call for the inclusion of people displaced by gradual or sudden environmental impacts within the refugee protection framework.

As discussed above, there is an ongoing debate and scepticism as to the direct link between climate change and displacement, but there is now mounting evidence which supports the plight of so-called 'climate change refugees' and demands attention from the international legal community. The term 'climate change refugee' is often used to describe those who will be forced to leave their homes because of climate change impacts. In this section, I will focus on the extent to which international refugee law may apply, and discuss why, by and large, it is an inappropriate framework for responding to the needs of the displaced.

The first official use of the term 'climate change refugee' was by Essam El-Hinnawi in a United Nations Environment Programme (UNEP) report, where he described people who are forced to leave their places of residence because of human or naturally induced environmental issues as 'environmental refugees'. El-Hinnawi was not trying to make a legal argument for the extension of refugee law to cover those displaced for environmental reasons, but instead was using the term to highlight the potentially devastating effects of unchecked development and pollution. Since then the term has been used in almost any discussion involving the impacts of climate change and forced migration. While those displaced internally (within their own countries) can be protected using the United Nations Guiding Principles on Internal Displacement mechanism, or even by the national law of their own countries, those displaced by environmental impacts and who are crossing or wish to cross their countries' borders currently have no legal basis for this type of movement in international law.

The relationship between climate change, natural disasters, and migration

What is the positive or negative impacts when climate change causes disasters and then bring migration number increases or decreases? The relationship between climatic shocks, natural disasters, and migration has received increasing attention in recent years and is quite controversial. One view suggests that climate change and its associated natural disasters increase migration. An alternative view suggests that climate change may only have marginal effects on migration. Knowing whether climate change and natural disasters lead to more migration is crucial to better understand the different channels of transmission between climatic shocks and migration and to formulate evidence-based policy recommendations for the efficient management of the consequences of disasters.

What are the positive and negative impacts when climate change causes natural disasters and migration attributes? I shall indicate as below:

On migration benefit aspect, it may include these such as: migration can help people cope with the adverse effects of climatic shocks by providing them with new opportunities and resources. Remittances from overseas migrants increase after disasters in their home countries and play an important role in mitigating the adverse effects of climatic shocks and natural disasters. Climatic factors, such as natural disasters or rainfall and temperature variations, may increase international migration through their effect on internal migration. Agricultural productivity represents one of the pathways that can explain the relationship between climatic shocks and migration.

However, climate change may also bring these disadvantages on migration benefit aspect, they may include such as: Public intervention both before and after disasters helps build resilience and can explain why migration responses differ according to different shocks. The migration response to disasters depends on the nature of the shock (slow vs rapid onset events), its severity, and the vulnerability of the affected people.Due to liquidity constraints, poor people might not be able to migrate in the aftermath of climatic shocks. Also, in developing countries, international migration due to disasters may be driven by highly educated people, which may foster brain drain in a vulnerable context.

Climate Change and the Migrant Crisis

What is climate change and migrant crisis ? It may include as below:

For India example, when climate change , it can influence India migrant decision. India has the first airport which is solely functioning on solar energy. The world can learn from India or China. The West has to stop dumping subsidized agar products into third world destroying local agar industry and pushing people into poverty. Western fisheries are just taking all fish from coasts of Africa. If these policies continue, europeans dont complain people coming to your countries. For afria example, Africa has tripled their population from 400 million to over 1.2 billion people in the past 40 years. Overpopulation, not climate change is their root problem. Africa now has 1 and quarter billion Africans living in some of the world's wort market places. This new lie (scheme) is a dreamed up scheme to import as many as they can into the first world market places, Europe, u.s., Australia, place them on welfare, make the tax payers foot the bill for all the goods and services they can consume to maximize annualized corporate profits making, and to turn them into citizens and have the tax payers pay to educate them so hopefully they will in the future expand taxes uptake for the government's. All paid for by the tax payers. you get to be absorbed genetically. So, it seems that climate change will bring more negative impact to migrants , when the country can attract many migrants choose to emigrate to the county to live, due to climate change infuences.

● Vulnerable countries number will increase when climate change become worse to influence human live as well as human needs to learn new skills to adapt difficult lives

The relationship between migration and the environment is not new. From the mid-19th century Great Irish Famine to the early 20th century Dust Bowl, we have many examples in history of people choosing or being forced to migrate because of changes in their physical environments. What is new now is that the world is grappling with the devastating impacts of climate change. With greater awareness came increased political recognition and there is now a widespread consensus on the need to address the adverse impacts of climate change on the migration of people now and in the future.

Climate migration is a reality in all parts of the world, however, the situation in what is known as "vulnerable countries" represents a particular challenge. Vulnerable countries are Least Developed Countries (LDCs), Landlocked Developing Countries (LLDCs) and Small Island Developing States (SIDS). In 2016, the 15 countries with the highest vulnerability to natural hazards were LDCs, LLDCs and SIDS. These countries are disproportionately affected by the negative impacts of climate change and are often least able to cope due to their structural constraints and geographical disadvantages. At the same time, they contribute the least to climate change. These countries are among the strongest advocates for more robust action on climate migration as they face very real challenges that affect all aspects of the daily lives of their populations.

Climate migration challenges take multiple forms in these vulnerable countries. In LDCs, the poorest and most vulnerable segment of the international community, climate change pressures can intersect with numerous development-related challenges as well as security issues. The combination of those factors often leads people to migrate in search of better or safer lives. For example, the Lake Chad Basin is currently experiencing grave environmental degradation, in a context where populations face the violence linked to the presence of groups such as Boko Haram. Migration patterns in that region have been reshaped due to these factors. Some LDCs such as Ethiopia and Bangladesh are sometimes saddled with the "double stress" of having to deal with internal climate migration, while also hosting large numbers of refugees from neighboring countries. LLDCs often have scarce water resources, further depleted by the impacts of climate change. This can create pressure on populations to migrate for better access to water. For example, nomadic pastoralists are often pushed to alter their traditional routes and travel further and for longer periods in search of water and land resources. Climate change is also affecting livelihoods, such as in Mongolia where extremely cold winters called dzud deplete nomadic livestock and destroy agriculture opportunities, pushing rural populations to migrate to urban centers.

SIDS are recognized as a special case for sustainable development as they face greater risk of marginalization due to their small size and remoteness. They also have fragile natural environments, and natural disasters such as storms and cyclones have a devastating impact on the population. The adverse impacts of climate change have contributed to the migration of thousands of people in SIDS in the last decade alone. One specific type of migration in this context is the planned relocation of people, where entire communities need to be moved, generally further inland, to escape climate change impacts such as coastal erosion. In Fiji, following Tropical Cyclone Winston in 2016, more than 60 villages were relocated to reduce people's exposure and vulnerability to further risks.

The current situation is clearly preoccupying and addressing the negative impacts of climate change on the migration of people in vulnerable countries should represent a priority now and for the future. We are moving towards a high level week of crucial political dialogues at the United Nations General Assembly in September 2019. In particular, the United Nations Climate Action Summit is a key opportunity to highlight the challenges of most vulnerable countries and put forward commitments and solutions to address climate migration issues.

On conclusion, riority should be given to mitigate the impacts of climate change and promote climate change adaptation in places where populations are at risk of forced migration. However, it is also clear that in some places, it will not be possible for populations to remain in situ and it is of utmost importance to think about how legal migration options can be offered to those migrants. It is also important to factor in the positive role that migrants can play in the fight against climate change, such as by facilitating remittances and transfer of skills and knowledge towards climate action. So, climate change influences human needs to change skills to adapt difficult lives.

How climate change impacts on developing countries economy ?

In fact, climate change will increase global temperature change rainfall patterns and will result in more frequent and severe floods and drought. Depending on future emission of greenhouse gases, global temperatures are likely to rise between 2 degree and 4 degree within the next century. The main impacts of climate change will however not be felt through higher temperatures, but through a change in the hydrological cycle. Rainfall is likely to increase around the poles and the tropics when in the sub-tropics average precipitation is likely to decrease. Not only the average annual or seasonal rainfall will change, there also be an increase in the number of extreme events resulting in most frequent and severe floods and droughts.

How does climate change influence to development countries? Climate change will influence any development countries on these several aspects. They include as below:

On trade influence hand, reducing emission levels from the developing world is extremely important. If current developments are continuing, for example, emissions from China and India both countries will save be much higher than the total emission form all Europe countries. Currently, the Europe is stimulating mitigation and transfer of clean technologies through the clean development mechanism (CDM). Although, it is still unclear what the mitigation potential of the (CDM) is, especially in India the investment is (CDM) projects is significant. However, the Europe should take a much wider approach. In developing countries a lot can be done in terms of increasing energy efficiency, land use change and agriculture. It is also important that developing countries are stimulated to choose a sustainable, low emission developed pathway. Choices for more sustainable, low emission technologies should be made early in the process. It seems that climate changing will encourage many countries will choose to do more environment protection related trading, e.g. researching how to invent environment protection new products to reduce our earth pollution between European and any developing countries, such as China and India etc.

On focus mitigation efforts in least developed countries on land use change, agriculture development aspect, in the least developed countries mitigation efforts should not focus on the energy or transport sector, but on agriculture and forestry. Agriculture is responsible for a relatively large percentage of the emissions in many developing countries, e.g. Africa, China, Malaysia, Hong Kong, Japan etc. In this sector there are many win options both reducing poverty and reducing greenhouse gas emissions. For example, improved water and nutrient management can sharply increase production efficiency and reduces at least the amount of emission per kg food produced. Agro-forestry reduces greenhouse gas emission through increased carbon storage and reduces poverty through diversifying the incomes of local communities.

However, in most developing countries, the main limitation in coping with the impacts of climate change is a lack of capacity. Besides a lack of capacity, in many developing countries, there is also a significant lack of data and knowledge on climate change impacts. Developing countries should be stimulated to improve data gathering and make existing data more easily available.However, no migration effort will stop the need for adaptation. Especially, the least developed countries, who have contributed little to the problem will suffer the most.

On business strategies for climate change aspect, nowadays, the valuation for clean-technology companies, have increased considerable and the corporate carbon footprint has become an important topic to be discussed how to solve among senior managers? How can firms profit from what they do to address climate change? Thus, a low-carbon economy is already especially in energy, transport and heavy industry.

If current climate science holds true and there is considerable uncertainty in the estimates, global greenhouse gas emissions should ideally decrease from today's levels by 90 percent as of 2050 year in order to certain global warming below two degrees centigrade. Hence, it seems global warmth challenge brings further any new energy potential development businesses. Due to environment scientists encourage us to be realized the necessary increase in carbon productivity and new low-carbon technologies that are necessary dramatically reduces energy consumption and direct greenhouse gas emissions will have to be developed and then implemented widely to avoid future serious global environment warmth caused climate changes and pollution challenges occurrence.

Reference

Hugo, G. (199). Environmental concerns and
International migration. International migration
Review., 30. Pp. 105-131.

Mendelsohn , R., (2013) " Climate Change And Economic Growth Commission On Growth And Development" working paper no 60.

Stern, N., (ed.) The economics of climate change: The Stern Review, Cambridge University Press, Cambridge, 2006, p.3.

Stern, N. (2007). The Economics Of Climate Change:
The Stern Review, Cambridge UK:
University Press.

UNHCR/WFP (United Nations High Commission For Refugees) World Food Program, 2009. Acute Malnutrition in protected refugee situation: A global strategy Geneva: UNHCR/WFP.

Zarocostas , J. 2011. Famine and disease threaten millions in drought hit horn of Africa. BMJ 343: doi: 10,1136/bmj.d4a4a <online 21 July 2011>.

CHAPTER NINE

Reason the transport supply and Tesco stores fresh sale cooperation may raise sale price

● This case concerns chain involved in the supply of fresh fruit and vegetables to Tesco stores cooperation challenge

The place(P) of the traditional marketing mix decides about channel intermediaries or middlemen to use an outdated, yet user friendly, term and the management of physical distribution. Placing products involves managing the process supporting the flow of goods or services from producers to consumers.

The process has sometimes been described as developing the best routes to market for a firm's products. Products must be made available in the right quantity, in the right location, and at the times when customers wish to purchase them. Marketing channels can perform an important role in the later stages of a value chain, in particular outbound logistic (e.g. order processing, storage and transportation); marketing and sales (e.g. market research, personal selling, sales promotion) and after sales service. However, it depends on which kinds of business to need outbound logistic, such as Tesco supermarket only needs ordering fresh fruit and vegetables from local farmers, then these foods need to be stored in refrigerate in warehouse and transport these foods to different supermarkets by vans. So, Tesco value chain only needs outbound logistic activity, but it does not need marketing and sales and after sale service to sell its fresh fruit and vegetables to its clients from its supermarkets (stores). In fact, Tesco stores

is such UK farmer's intermediaries which can add value by breaking bulk. This might involve purchasing in large quantities of fruits and vegetables from UK local farmers and then selling smaller, more manageable, to keep volumes of fresh food stock in warehouses, then its vans will deliver these fresh fruits and vegetables to different stores daily. Discrepancies of fruit foods quantity are reduced by Tesco (intermediary) who provides every store clients with individual preferable fresh foods items that suit their needs daily. Tesco stores can offer superior knowledge of a target market compared with farmers, for example by ensuring which kinds of vegetables or fruits foods numbers are stocked in every store to match the economic and lifestyle needs of Tesco store shoppers who live in the area. Probably the most important gaps between Tesco store shoppers and UK local farmers in channel management are indicated at those of location and time. A location gap occurs owing to the geographic separation of farmers and the store shoppers of their fresh fruit and vegetables foods. UK farmers generally want to grow their fruits and vegetable food in one central location (farming), but farmers' food buyers typically want to buy their growing foods locally. A time gap arises when the UK local farmers' fresh foods buyers want to buy whose fresh growing foods at a time when a UK local farmer may considerate it inconvenient to make the available. UK local farmers may like to grow fresh fruits and vegetable foods at night from 8:00 PM to 12:00PM, then who will collect these fresh foods
from 5:00 AM to 7:00 in the morning, but their buyers may want to buy in the evenings or at weekends afternoon. Tesco stores (intermediary) need to facilitate vans to transport these fresh fruits and vegetables foods from farmers' farming to its one central warehouse to deliver to different stores to sell the budget numbers of different kinds of foods to every local store consumers more exactly (Adrian, P. 2012).

Tesco stores is one of the world's largest retailers, it has social responsibility to protect fresh fruit and vegetable to sell to clients. It had attempted to predict customer behavior about hope much fresh fruit and vegetable and what kinds of fresh fruit and vegetable whose consumers will buy from data statistic in warehouse. It aims to reduce excess fruit and vegetable stocks in warehouse to cause perishable. In the winter might have seen choice reduced to basic items such as potatoes, cabbage, apples, supplemented by canned fruit and vegetables. Look in a Tesco supermarket today, and clients may find difficult to tell the season of the year or the distance from the countryside, simple based on the fruit and vegetables with are on display. In UK supermarket sector is intensely competitive, and has seen continuous innovation in the way it seeks to satisfy customers' needs. As consumers have become wealthier, the supermarkets realized that buyers would no longer be content with the staple foods such as cabbage and potatoes in the depths of winter-significant numbers of them now wanted excitement on a plate, and all year round. Furthermore, if they were planning a menu, they wanted to be sure that when they went to their local supermarket.

By and large, supermarkets have been key drivers of the value for the groceries that they sell. They have been close to their customers and identified their changing needs. They have built confidence with their customers, who can trust freshness and provenance of food they sell and the reliability of supply. It is therefore the supermarkets who have gone seeking sources of supply, rather than growers aggressively seeking to sell the produce that they have available. Before, the development of very large supermarket chains, retailers were more
fragmented. They did not have the power or resources to innovate with new product lines which they could then commission a grower to produce. Today, supermarket such as Tesco invest heavily in their food technology laboratories, and can then go to suppliers and place large orders with exacting standards with regard to price, quality, and delivery. Above all else, supermarkets have put themselves at the center of a slick distribution system which connects an international networks of growers through transport networks of trucks, ships and planes to put fresh produce in their network of stores, every day, all year around. The efficiency of the logistics, and the bargaining power of the supermarkets has often led to the price being charged at a British supermarket being lower than the price changed in supermarkets thousands of miles away where fruit and vegetables were grown. Tomatoes grown in Bulgaria and sold in Britain can be cheaper in Britain in local Bulgarian shops. The bizarre situation has occurred where the supermarkets import apples from France to be sold in Kent, the traditional home of British apple growing, plums from Poland to be sold in the grown product in Lincolnshire. Supermarkets argue that sourcing from overseas is not just an issue of cost saving more importantly, the supermarkets seek a continuity of supplies from large growers who can guarantee to deliver a specified quantity at a specified quantity at a specified time and place. The supermarkets capable of achieving this. British supermarkets are among the most efficient in the world, and their desire

to ensure that customers can always get what they want may explain the mass transport of food. Local farmers' market may could environmentally friendly, but they rarely guarantee a continuity of supplies. As part of their drive for efficiency, supermarkets have a tendency to move food , such potatoes could being transported several hundred miles between distribution centers before they end up on a supermarket shelf just a few miles from where potatoes were grown. The environmental campaigning group Sustain has estimated that the average children travels 2,000 between the farm where it was grown and the supermarket shelf and furthermore the distance products travel from farm to end customer increased by an estimated 25 per cent between 1980 year and 2007 year (Priesnitz 2007).

Global warming had become an important issue with many clients and there was growing concern that supermarkets' practice of transporting fresh produce long distances around the world was irresponsibly adding to greenhouse gas emissions. Hence, distance travelled was one of value chain factor Terso supermarket needs to consider their fruit and vegetables food to keep fresh in refrigerate to transport to retailers to sell in UK. The most contentious food miles are clocked up by fresh fruit and vegetables flow in by plane from overseas. Although, air freighted produce accounted for less than 1 per cent of total UK food miles, it was the fastest growing way of moving foods around. One response By Tesco was to introduce a greatest proportion of local produce. To achieve this, it placed buyers and marketing teams in the regions in order to get a clear picture of local markets and to develop relationships with suppliers. By 2007 year, Tesco claimed to have 7,000 regional lines from throughout the UK, which were promoted as local produce, supporting local growers and reducing greenhouse gas emissions. Throughout its history, Tesco has demonstrated its ability to listen to what customers want, and this has been true in respect of its distribution system. The weaknesses of commodity systems are particularly for major customers, such as Mc Donalds, commodity systems do not lead to reliability in supply, quality, quantity or price nor high rates of innovation on which they can differentiate their offer from their competitors. The opportunity and challenge of fresh food product differentiation, so Tesco stores need to innovation to give rise to a number of strategic options to keep vegetables and fruits to be fresh in the short time to sell full numbers. If a firm, such as Tesco is the lowest cost producer than commodity market strategy can be an attractive strategic option. As Tesco stores fresh food sale that it's larger competitors shall find difficult to copy. Otherwise, Smaller size stores can sometimes be a competitive advantage.

Tesco stores (fresh food retailer) need to co-operate with suppliers and fresh food growers to align the whole chain to the changing needs of consumers. The food chain strategy aims to deliver superior value to specific groups of customers. Tesco stores work closely with its fresh food suppliers to develop specific products for each range. Both the supplier and growers understand the Tesco marketing strategy and their role in the innovation process. Tesco is actively seeking new chain ideas and is prepared to pay for such efforts. From a primary producer and supplier perspective the range of brands enables Tesco to work with suppliers to market the total crop .

CHAPTER TEN

Reasons of societal marketing orientation may help body shop to raise sale price

What is the difference between production orientation and societal marketing orientation and sales orientation to body shop ?

Critically assess the extent to which whether Body Shop to be a truly marketing oriented organization throughout its 30 years history.The body shop international power line carrier (the body shop) was founded by Dame Anita Roddick in the England in 1976. It sold personal beauty care products, such as baby and child specific products, bath and shower and colour cosmetics, deodorants, skin care, hair care, fragrances, sun care etc skin health products to provide human body benefits. Nowadays, the body shop was skin and body care manufacturer and retailer operating in 55 countries with over 2,100 stores. It had 42 exclusive outlets in Hong Kong. It's missions were to dedicate to pursuit of social and environment change to meaningfully contribute to local, national and international communities in which trade to passionately campaign for the protection of the environment, human and civil rights and against animal testing and to make fun, passion and care part of our daily lives (Adrian, P. 2012).

There are five main marketing orientations of which a company will adopt one. This will determine the way it interacts with the customer. Such as product orientation suggests that a company focuses inwards looking at what it is capable of, rather than the needs and wants of the client; sales orientation is based upon selling existing products with a turnover sale numbers relationship marketing orientation recognizes the value of repeat business over, not only with customers but suppliers as well; societal marketing orientation is relatively new in the scheme of things but suggests on top of meeting the needs and wants of the customer and the organization there is the societies interests to be looked and marketing orientation is based around the needs and wants of a customer to meet business objectives and it assumes that a sale depends on a customer's decision to purchase a product or provide a service.

● What is marketing two levels meaning ?

Marketing can be seen at two levels, the first level is such as a business philosophy, marketing puts customers at the center of an organization's consideration and which is reflected in basic values , such as the requirement to understand and respond to customers' needs and the necessary to search constantly for new market opportunity. In a truly marketing oriented organization, these values are instilled in all employees and should influence their behavior without any need for prompting. The personnel manager would have a selection policy that recruited staff who could fulfil the needs of customers rather than simply minimizing the wage bill in any marketing oriented organization. The other level is techniques of marketing also include pricing, the design of channels of distribution and new product development.

● What are the three components of market orientation ?

The assessing the nature and importance of market orientation for large firms, such as body shop. The three components of market orientation could be analytically separated. The components of market orientation organization include the first component is the customer orientation, it means an organization must have a thorough understanding of its target buyers, so that it can create a product of superior value to give client benefits ; the second component is the competitor orientation, it means any firm should look at how well its competitors are able to satisfy buyers' needs. It should understand the short term strengths and weaknesses and long term capabilities and strategies of current and potential competitors as well as the third component is to develop marketing plans that are not acted upon by people who are capable of delivering promises made to customers and a marketing orientation organization requires that the organization draws upon and integrates its human and physical resources effectively and adapts them to meet client's needs. Otherwise, a production and sales orientation may be appropriate to firms at certain stages in the evolution of markets. Where the dominant business environment is based on the need for good production planning above all, the company that does this best will achieve the greatest overall business success.

It is either production orientation, it means organizations that produce what they imagined consumers wanted, rather than what they actually wanted. Planning for full utilization of capital equipment are often seen as more important than ensuring that equipment is used to provide goods and services that people actually wants. Production-oriented firms generally aim for efficiency in production rather than effectiveness in meeting customer's needs . It is either or selling orientation, it means advertising, sales promotion and personal selling techniques are used to emphasize product differentiation and brands and it does not focus on satisfying client needs or desire new product offerings and production led. Hence, one market orientation organization needs to focus on satisfying clients' needs profitably by these marketing mix, such as product, price, place, physical evidence, processed, people and promotion. Anyway ,Market orientation implied that body shop , which ought seek information about clients, such as current and future needs and took action based this information (client orientation); it ought seek information about competitors' current strengths and weaknesses and their long term strategies and took actions based on these information (competitor orientation) ; it ought coordinate the actions taken by sharing clients and competitors information internally (intra-firm communication).

● What is the three components of market orientation ?

The three components of market orientation meant social marketing and understanding boarder concerns and ethical environmental, legal and social context of marketing activities and programs. The cause and effects of marketing clearly beyond the company and the consumer to society as whole. New terms humanistic marketing and ecological marketing were suggested to societal marketing concept.

● What is the social marketing concept ?

The social marketing concept holds that the organization's task is to determine the needs, wants and interests of target markets and to deliver the desired satisfactions more effectively and
efficiently than competitors and the society's welling being, such as body shop had achieved sales and profit gains by adopting and practicing a form of the societal marketing concept called cause related marketing.

● DISCUSSION

Body Shop is marketing orientation organization in 30 years.Critically assess the extent to which I consider Body Shop to be a truly marketing oriented organization throughout its 30 years history . It seemed body shop had achieved cause-related marketing as an opportunity to enhance their corporate reputation, raised brand awareness, increased customer loyalty and built sales. It's corporate values were composed of five core values. The first one was to oppose animal testing. The opposing animal testing for both cosmetic products and ingredients began in 1976 years.

In the 1980 year and 1990 year, who successfully campaigned with animal protection groups to change the UK and European laws to support the development products were tried on human volunteers. Along with the development of technology testing had played a leading role to protect the rights of both human and animals . The second one was to support community trade, it initiated the trade not aid objective of creating trade to help people in the third world utilizing their resources to their own needs. This reflects communities needed a fair price for natural ingredients who purchased from these often marginalized countries. The third one was to activate self esteem. Women were the main customers and employees in the body shop. The fourth one was to defend human rights. The body shop had long campaign on human rights, highlighting abuses and increasing the global awareness of issues by making full use of the geographic advantages of their shops and supporting other human rights organizations. The last one was protect our plant. In 2001 year, huge campaign against global warming was hosted by the body shop and green peace, who advocated the use of recyclable source and materials (Adrian, P. 2012). Although profits were an essential element of long run survival in body shop and it was likely to be overall corporate and marketing objectives, but body shop seemed more to be required level of profits rather than profit that there were many other objectives, which might pursue through its pricing strategies . For example, if body shop wanted to maximize market share or simply survive, a different set of prices would be delivered than if the objectives were to maximize profits. Hence, body shop ought to see viewpoint the marketing side of pricing and it ought not to see viewpoint the production / supply side of pricing if it was a truly marketing oriented organization.

The key inputs for body shop to make pricing decision whether it was marketing oriented or productive / supply oriented included production objectives or marketing objectives, demand or supply numbers were considered cost or sale price and competitors or clients consideration factors, such as beauty skin care products in competitive markets demand, i.e. To decide the price whether customers are willing and able to pay is a major consideration in the selection of pricing strategies and levels of demands . Hence, body shop ought to consider demand numbers , it ought not consider production / supply numbers if it was a truly marketing oriented organization. For example, since most of the body shop's factories were still located in the UK, where wages and salaries were much higher than in Asia, so UK itself sale product prices were higher than that from Asia itself sale product prices.

I think Body Shop was a truly marketing oriented organization more than production/supply oriented organization throughout its 30 years history. In fact, Body Shop was experiencing market level growth. It could expand its sales market in Europe, America, Middle East, Asia and Africa etc different countries. It seemed that it had attempted to carry on marketing research to decide to choose which countries would have more client numbers to demand to buy its personal care products, then it would follow the countries' estimated client numbers to produce its products to sell to the countries. So, it was why some Asia countries sold its bath and shower and skin and hair care and colour cosmetics products more than its fragrances products, such as Hong Kong young people were more acceptable to use bath and show and color cosmetic and skin and hair care products more than fragrances products . It seemed that Hong Kong Body Shop sold fragrance products numbers were less than bath and shower and color cosmetics etc. products. Nowadays, I think the personal beauty care products new businesses which planned to entry this market was more difficult. It was possible than Body Shop was a famous personal beauty care products sale company, it had owned many clients too many years. So , it caused barriers to any new personal beauty care product competitors felt difficult to entry this market .Furthermore, Body Shop had build strong buyer and seller power to increase clients had more confident to use its products, it was possible that who felt its different kind of products could give more health to their skin or body more than other similar personal beauty care products. Moreover, I believe Body Shop had attempted to carry on technological experimenting to aim to build different countries' clients had more confident to use its products forever.

In conclusion, it seemed that Body Shop was truly marketing oriented organization more than productive/ supply oriented organization oriented organization throughout its 30 years history.

Any companies need to consider the social responsibility during which are the pursuits of profit and meeting the needs of wider group of stakeholders incompatible. Without this self interest, there will be little motivation for firms to provide better services, workers couldn't earn better salaries and clients couldn't aspire for a high level of consumption. Hence, self interest which helps markets work more effectively for the benefits of all. Hence, companies should adopt a code of behavior and conduct and ethical behavior which would not influence any stakeholders groups' benefits to pursuit their profit honestly. Corporate social responsibility is a form of corporate self regulation integrated into a business model. It aims to give responsibility for corporate actions and to encourage a positive impact on the environment and stakeholders including consumers, employees, investors, communities and others and it is titled to aid an organization's mission as well as guide to what the company can give the best benefits to serve its customers. I shall use body shop company as one example to judge whether what extent are the pursuits of profit and meeting the needs of wider groups of stakeholders will be incompatible.

In fact, body shop could adopt a code of behavior and conduct and ethical behavior which would not influence any stakeholders groups' benefits to pursuit their profit honestly. Such as, one of the major and most successful initiatives which body shop used an effective supply chain for their products and body shop made use of their sustainable chain supply strategy to ensure that there was the promotion and the maintenance of the social ethical behavior in its business. Hence, it seemed that body shop could be compatible to achieve an effective supply chain to deliver to different countries' stores to meet clients who had more need to buy different kinds of skin care products to provide them to choose to buy in the reasonable price choices in the short time. It is therefore in the best practices and interests for body shop to reach out to the communities in their businesses to provide raw materials to help the manufacturers of the beauty products. It also partook in the development of the market for such small scale suppliers. In many cases the body shop tried to outsource its raw materials to its customers. This had ensured the sustainability of its customer base this included it's sensitivity to its environment and the required standards of the labor practices of its partners. Hence, it seemed that body shop could be compatible to help its partners to earn profits and any countries' partners could provide more job chances to unemployed people to work from body shop's outsourcing strategy.

Hence, this had been developed by the body shop by including strategies, such as third party logistic providers and intermediaries in which who had no ownership. The body shop was a multinational company also adopted trading to purchasing approach where it shifted from short term where focus of buying articles to long term focus of fewer suppliers. This was an attempt of it to develop quality products where prices were also fair and affordable to sell to different countries' clients. It seemed that body shop could be compatible to sell reasonable prices of products to it's clients. Moreover, it had included in its strategies the aspect of business promotion using catalogues. For the same reason, it had been involved in printing of catalogues which were given out to the clients with their purchases. It was important to note that it' catalogues always contained all it's information descriptions and any person who purchased it's products was bound to receive the explanation of all it's product. This was an attempt of it to develop quality products where prices were also fair and affordable to sell to different countries' clients. It seemed that body shop could be compatible to provide clear information description in catalogues to let whose clients to know what it's different kinds of style body skin care products ingredients and benefits were , then who could compare it's products to other competitors to decide to buy or not buy fairly.

In Oct. 2007 the campaign for safe cosmetic products, in which 25 multinational companies participated, tested 33 brand name lipsticks and found one-third of the sampled exceeded the limit of lead allowed in confectionery. The affected brands included L'Oreal and Christian Dior. A definite effect would be that consumers would be more concerned regarded the ingredients of products who used, which was likely to have an effect on cosmetics and skin care products were released to capture share. It seemed body shop needed to consider its beauty personal care products were the most ensure to own organic ingredients to let any countries clients (stakeholder) to meet their body health care needs (Adrian, P. 2012).

On the health and natural aspect, body shop had health and safe responsibility to consumers. Although, I felt who had considered this issue because it had 30 years history to operate this business and it had not received any serious negative complaints damage its health product image from clients before. However, with consumers were increasingly informed and were educated, who were now more demanding for more information regarding products and were becoming more aware of health issue. Products with organic ingredients and natural ingredients, such as tea and plants were gaining popular. Furthermore, consumers were looking for healthier substitutes to seemingly unhealthy products, such as color cosmetics. Hence, body shop began to sell the reducing numbers, it was possible due to clients compared it's body care products quality to the other competitors and who felt it's product's ingredients existed some poor ingredients to cause every one's body to be unhealthy.

Hence, it's productive processing was very important. It seemed that body shop could be compatible to consider its individual client body skin health issue whether after who had used it's body skin care products to have skin hurt or skin pain feeling. In conclusion, to judge what extent are the pursuits of profit and meeting the needs of wider groups of stakeholders incompatible for any individual business, it is depended on whether the company's any stakeholders, such as employees, clients, suppliers, partners, society (communities) etc. who will have positive or negative influence from it. I feel that it will be incompatible if the company give negative influence to any one of its stakeholder. Hence, if any one company's at least one stakeholder who felt who had negative influence due to it did business to relate to whom unwillingly, then it's pursuit of profits aim would be incompatible to meet it's needs of its any one of stakeholder. Such as body shop will give positive influence to its all stakeholders. Hence, I feel it is compatible extent to pursuit of profit and meeting the needs of its wider groups of stakeholders definitely.

I feel that Nestle company has managed to sustainable reconcile to pursuit profits and meeting the needs of its wider groups of stakeholders two aims compatibly. Nestle was the world's largest food and beverage company. Nestle in the United States, which represented seven operating across the USA country and it was the first expanded effort in USA and achievement tied to Nestle 's global sustainability principle and commitment. Nowadays, It served 97% of American householders and Nestle 's mission was to lead the industry in nutrition, health and wellness and to create a more sustainable future. Instead of it's mission was to pursuit of profits aim, it had also achieved specific sustainability commitment and progress in the categories of nutrition, environmental impact and water use, social impact, rural development and responsible sourcing to meet the needs of it's wider of groups of stakeholders' aim. On the nutrition, health and wellness aspect, Nestle met the needs to its stakeholder (clients), such as, Nestle rolled out new portion guidance tools and launched an educational campaign and balance your plate to help consumers build nutritious and delicious and convenient meals that met the dietary guidelines for Americans; Nestle also reduced sodium content in many of its most popular brands, such as Stouffer's and DiGiorno and committed to further reduce sodium content by 10 percent in products that did not meet the Nestle; Nestle also reduced sugar content, such as ninety six percent of Nestle 's children's products met the Nestle criteria for low sugar and by the end of 2014 year, 100 percent of children's products would meet these criteria as well as Nestle also removed trans-fat content, such as Nestle committed to reach zero food and beverage products with trans-fat originating to use as functional ingredients by 2016 year. It seemed that Nestle had considered its food and beverage production content whether these content would have negative influence to its stakeholder (clients) nowadays (Adrian, P. 2012).

On the environmental impact aspect, Nestle reduced waste during it's food and beverage products were producing. As part of its commitment to eliminate all forms of waste, Nestle reduced 44 percent of waste per ton of product since 2010 year in the USA five factory locations reached zero waste to landfill status by the end of 2013 year; Nestle also considered responsible packaging responsibility, such as Nestle Waters North America led the USA bottled water industry in light weighting packaging, in part by reducing the plastic content of its 1/2 liter bottles by 60 percent since 1994 year. Since 2003 year alone, more than 3.3 billion pounds of plastic had been saved by Nestle as well as Nestle also adopted responsible sourcing, such as Nestle Purina Pet Care implemented responsible sourcing guidelines for seafood that align with Nestle 's global responsible sourcing guidelines, working with experts to track suppliers and contribute to healthier ecosystem. In 2013 year, Nestle also reached an important target for palm oil, with 100 percent of palm oil now Round table on sustainable palm oil certified. It seemed that Nestle also considerate whether environment would have negative influence occurrence during it's production (Adrian, P. 2012).

On social impact aspect, Nestle supported local communities, such as Nestle in USA donated more than $2.3 million dollars to support local United Way organizations; It also provided disaster relief, such as Nestle waters donated more than 685,000 bottled of water and Nestle Purina contributed more than 60,000 pounds of pet food and 41,000 pounds of cat little to local shelters across the USA for disaster relief as well as it grew supplier diversity, such as Nestle works with over 4,100 small, minority, women and veteran owned businesses to help to spur local economies. It seemed that Nestle also considerate social needs. Thus, it is seemed Nestle company have managed to sustainable reconcile these two aims to pursuit profit as well as it also could gave positive influence to its stakeholders. Such as consumer could feel safe to enjoy to eat Nestle company's health foods; societies could be reduced unemployment from its outsourced assistance job to partners; natural environment could be reduced pollution from its productive protection. Hence, it was not actually neglect its shareholders' benefits during it was doing business as the same time (Adrian, P. 2012).

What are basic lessons in marketing that the Body Shop might have taken on board in its early years in order to improve its chances of long term success?

The body shop is a global manufacturer and retailer of naturally inspired , ethically produced beauty and cosmetics products. Founded in the UK in 1976 year by Dame Anita Roddick, who now have 2,133 stores in 55 countries with a range of over 1,200 products in Europe, America, Middle East, Asia and Africa. However, the body shop has not entered the China market. It takes a strong position on activism, ethical business, human rights and environmentalism in a global perspective. The body shop is banned in China because cosmetics sold there have to be tested on animals, according to Roddick. In, 2006 when it was bought by the French cosmetics company L'Oreal which is a big player in China. China has launched scientific developing strategy for future the current policies of advocating. Hence, it is the perfect time for the body shop to enter China market. However, prior to that, as an independent member of the L'Oreal family, the body shop has to make decisions on differentiation marketing strategies, market segmentation and marketing position (Adrian, P. 2012).

It might have taken two purposes to body shop marketing in its early years in order to improve its chances from short term to long term success. The short term objective was to generate more sales for the body shop. Through, the introduction of a new service, the market up class, it was hoped that clients could try and experience the body shop cosmetic products. Positive experience of using its products could then be developed through their trial using the market up class. It was estimated that this positive experience could push up the sales.

The long term objective was to educate the belief of the body shop to the young potential clients, so that who would become those who preferred natural cosmetic products and were loyal to the body shop in the future. Objectives could provide the starting point for marketing plans and strategies and should be specific targets that are obtained but also challenging. Specific, measurable, agreed, realistic and time related objectives might be taken to body shop to improve early years in chances in long term success. It seemed that Hong Kong was one good market for body shop to satisfy an unfulfilled customers needs to pursue body shop investment chance. Therefore, the objective were to push up sales and built a loyal customer basis for the future. For example, Hong Kong was one young student clients growth market to body shop. In the past, one cosmetic products market statistic was indicated that the colour cosmetic retail value had been increasing from 2002 year, HK$938.3 million dollars to 2007 year, HK$1,132,3 million dollars, so percentage was increased to 5.12% . (Adrian, P. 2012).

It seemed Hong Kong might be one good skin cosmetic care products developed market to this body shop in early years. The another factor might improve body shop long term success factor was whether body shop had attempted to analyze direct competition. The body shop's direct competition was not from the name brand like Dior, Chanel or Olay, but rather the less well known brands, from Japan or Korea. Along with the great impact of Korean fashion, many Korean cosmetics brands like Missha and the Face shop had already established shops in China. These two brands also promoted their natural ingredients and target the young customer segment as what the body shop products competition concept could be offered to a market to satisfy a want or need and offered five levels, which were the core benefits, basic product, expected product, augmented product and potential product. Each level added more customer value and the five constitute client value hierarchy products of these three brands were all using natural ingredients and simple and natural in packaging. The body shop , however, differentiated itself at the top levels of the five product and transformations the products might undergo in the future.

Marketing management and planning was essential to body shop, it was the implementation of strategies to achieve long run profitability to body shop and growth. When body shop was looking at how it would achieve this in early years in order to improve the chances long term success, its two keys points to consider are:

What was body shop man activity at a particular time? And how it would reach its goals? It might design a strategy that insured a consistent approach to offer its skin care products to raise competition in mind the skin care products changing market. These included product line, distribution methods, marketing communication and pricing. For example, achieving marketing research to Hong Kong and China skin care products market to analyze what were these factors to influence these country people who felt needs to buy its skin care products: Such as internal factors include personality, motivation, learning, perception and attitude; external factors included culture, social class, reference groups , family and personal influences and situational factors included time, income, mobility and availability. The reason was because due to consumers bought skin care products to protect whose skin (core benefits) and their expectations if who were willing to pay more basic product. To enhance the product level, body shop skin health product needed emphasize that skin products were natural. Products of the body shop offered the same effective and natural and flavor and unique corporate values. Body shop was mostly natural (augmented level). Far more than the visible products, the shop shop's unique corporate values create the potential value to fulfil customer's desire of making a better health world. It's good corporate desire citizenship went beyond supplying rational and emotional benefits. Body shop might enter China market to improve long term success. The body shop divided its markets to include overseas Pacific Europe, America , Australia and New Zealand, Middle East, Africa and local UK countries. Adrian, P.(2012) indicated that a sampling questionnaire survey was conducted among 200 consumers, ranging from 18 to 50 ages in May 2006, a total of 170 valid responses that were used for analysis. Among the 170 responses, 66% were females. The findings were:

(1) About 60 % hoped that cosmetics could be a symbol of being environmental friendly.

(2) 90% would choose products made of natural ingredients.

(3) 90% spent less than 300 RMB on cosmetics and skin care products quarterly.

(4) 83% Chinese youth (age range from 18 to 25 ages) were innovators and conscious of environment.

Hence, the body shop might take a share of potential market in China. It should launch its products among younger cosmetic industry were young females who chased beauty and were willing to spend money on it. So, packaging was one of the vital factors in attracting client. The body shop took a unique approach by choosing simple packaging. The package was not made for mature women. It was made for young female students, who could enjoy on international brand at an inexpensive cost. The body shop was not only to meet young people's demand for beauty , but the demand of being responsible to environment and human rights. Hence, the target market of the body shop should focus on young people ageing from 15 ages to 30 ages. Hence, body shop might take marketing research in Hong Kong and China market to have more confident to invest in these market to improve more success.

Next, Whether body shop might achieve price strategy to improve to raise success chance. An assumption is when the individual client is considering the price of any a body shop's beauty skin health product. Economic theory suggests that the customer will act in a totally rational economic manner, such that body shop's every client total utility (or satisfaction) is maximized. In deciding whether try or not try body shop's product, which totally rational consumer will carefully equate whether ought to buy or ought not buy body shop's product at the asking price set will maximizing whose utility. In making judgment, the economist assumes that the consumer has perfect information about both the prices and utility of all the other competitive products in the market and that price is the only consideration in choice. Clearly there are unrealistic assumptions. Price could be determined easily when a target market was identified. (Adrian, P. 2012)

From survey indicated 64% of the 170 responses spent less than 1000 RMB on cosmetics and skin care every quarter and 24% of their expenditure was between 100 RMB and 300 RMB on cosmetics an skin care. This number could not be ignored if a cosmetics company wanted to enter this large market and be a leader. For the younger generation, the prices of the products could not be high. The price of these main competitors ranges from 10RMB to 200 RMB. The prices in Hong Kong have higher than that in the USA or the UK. And the consumer's purchasing power in mainland China is much lower than that of Hong Kong . Hence, body shop should adopt a price range in China which was similar to that of the USA or the UK rather than of Hong Kong. Once the body shop established greatly reduced and the capability of price adjustment would be achieved accordingly.

Further, body shop might have chain stores selling channel strategy to attempt to achieve long term success. Sample survey revealed that supermarket was for Chinese to purchase skin care and cosmetics. 120 out of the 170 responses hoped that who could choose products from the chain stores in the future, which suggested that the body shop should build up its own stores was regarded as cares about corporate culture and corporate image. It insisted on selling in its own stores rather than setting up counters in a shopping mall. The stores of body shop could be found easily worldwide because of stores were importance in this competitive buyer. Hence, in China, its appearance should be same as worldwide. Some housewives joined the body shop as sales agent and hold sales parties for other housewives. The sales channel allowed the body shop to reach out to more clients by bringing the store directly into client's homes. This would be a totally new method of marketing in China, but it offered a good opportunity for women to choose products and share feedback in a relaxed atmosphere. This fresh concept could attract female consumers. Nowadays, students in China could only obtain famous skin care products and cosmetics brands from campus agents, as who could not afford the products sold over the counters. It was a major problem that agents could not guarantee the ingredients and the quality of the goods. If the body shop could hold small parties to share products and opinions, that would be a good way to boost sales among students. Hence, body shop might take price strategy to Hong Kong and china market to predict whether what price who could accept to raise more confident to invest to this market to improve more success.

Further, body shop might also have promotion strategy to attempt to achieve long term success. The body shop adopted environmental friendly manufacturing, opposed abuses of human rights and was accountable for its actions. The unique values attracted numbers of media groups in many countries. This results in its establishing a good reputation without any advertisements. The body shop also joined numerous social causes, which substitute advertisements. In China, however, it was totally different. In this brand new market, most people were out aware of this company. If it carried on a marketing promotion of no commercials it was impossible to reach a high market share. Hence, commercial advertisements were needed in China. The body shop could use this advertisement to give on impression that women should care about their well being both mentally and physically and it had created a sexy grand with simple packaging and without objectifying women. Many brands reach customers directly by colorful commercials and show their products in movies and TV play series. For the sakes of brand image, some movies about human rights , environmental protection and animal protection could be chosen by the body shop as carriers for particular commercial as most of the audiences were well educated, well paid and environmentally concerned.

The target consumers of the body shop aged from 20 to 40 ages were energetic , knowledgeable and environmentally concerned. The body shop could give some lectures on makeup or skin care on campuses to raise feeling among students. To reach brand awareness and high brand loyalty , some samples should be given to students by experience marketing approach. Hence, body shop might take promotion to Hong Kong and China schools to let many young people to know why who needed to buy skin care products to protect their body skin to persuade who felt more needs. In conclusion, the body shop was famous for creating a niche market sector for naturally inspired skin care and cosmetic products through it's unique corporate values worldwide. The significance of the body shop's early entry into China market were strongly proposed. Once the body shop decided to enter the China market, the relevant marketing strategies and management should be implemented, such as the market segmentation and market positioning with the proper consideration of Chinese consumers should be studied in order to win the mind share of potential Chinese customers with the right marketing strategies. Overall, the findings of market survey and theoretical analysis strategy support the feasibility of the body shop's early entry into China market.

CHAPTER ELEVEN

Reason of sales of ready meals in supermarket may help cooking food raise sale price

Case study change in the marketing environment on sales of ready meals to supermarket, such as Walt Mark strategy ?

Using an appropriate framework of analysis, briefly summarize the effects of change in the marketing environment on sales of ready meals. Although, previously dismissed and a poor substitute for real cooking and ready meal sales have grown rapidly in recent years in many western developed countries, such as UK, France or Germany. But, Ready meal manufacturers ready to respond to a changing marketing environment. Due to one big change in recent year has been growing demand for ready prepared meals bought from a supermarket. An analysis of the reasons for the growth in the ready prepared meals markets indicates the effects of boards factors in the marketing environment on the size of a particular market. In fact, this food market is changing to drive the growth in the ready meals market, but there are differences in the food market potential between countries. The effect of change in the marketing environment on sales of ready meals, such as technology has played a big role in the growing take up of ready meals and new technologies have allowed companies to develop ready meals which preserve taste and texture, which still making them easy to use by the consumer.

Furthermore, great advances in distribution management, in particular the use of information technology to control inventories, has allowed fresh, chilled ready meals to be effectively and efficiently distributed without the need for freezing or added preservatives. Ready meals particularly appeal to single householders, which individual family members tend to eat at different times, so family meals together remains stronger in many continental European countries than in the UK individual ready meals. Young people have lost the ability to cook creatively, as cookery has been reduced in importance in the school, so young clients group will rise to buy ready meals from supermarket. Marketing can be seen as a system that must respond to environmental change. A food market can be defined as a meeting place for stakeholder (consumers) and sellers. Food market can be set up in a supermarket or restaurants. A food market consists of the individual's target taste, such as older group, family group, young group or business clients who are actual or potential caters of a restaurant meals or supermarket package of foods. Grocery stores (supermarkets) have an influence of meals (fast cooked food) outlets in low income urban areas, which has contributed to the income in access to healthy foods. An organization's marketing environment means the individuals, organizations, and forces external to the marketing management's ability to develop and maintain successful exchanges with its customers. The marketing environment to ready meal manufacturers had three levels.

Firstly, it includes the micro environment, it describes those elements that impinge directly on the ready meal manufacturers themselves, so the micro environment of ready meal manufacturers which include business clients who have direct contact, such as restaurants, supermarkets and individual clients who have direct contact. Otherwise, supermarket shoppers, restaurant clients and food supply competitors who have no direct contract to ready meal manufacturers, so who won't include in food market micro environment to ready meal manufacturers. Secondly, it includes the macro environment, it describes things that are beyond the immediate environment but can nevertheless affect an organization, so the macro environment of ready meal manufacturers which include the export countries‘ economies forces, such as unemployment ratio, GDP; technological forces, such as the export countries' factories food productive technology; social/ cultural forces, such as the export countries‘ people taste acceptance; political/legal forces, such as the export countries' import food quota numbers. Thirdly, it includes the internal environment, it describes ready meal manufacturers‘ employees and equipment and finance and functional responsibilities.

Environment means everything outside influences the person, in contrast with individual or personal variables . The effects of change in the marketing environment on sales of ready meals can be analyzed by creating healthy food and eating environment changing factor and supermarket technological changing factor as below:

The ready meal manufacturers could not ignore threats to the natural ecological environment change Due to the food companies could have technology to manufacture good taste cooked ready meals to provide to supermarkets to sell. Thus, it might influence the consumers to decide whether restaurants or supermarkets or ready meals suppliers who could provide the most reasonable price and taste to satisfy whose eating needs every day. Thus, it caused the growing demand for ready prepared cooked meals bought from supermarkets. Due to it was possible that consumers felt to eat ready cooked meals in expensive restaurants or who did not like to buy foods to cook from food suppliers or who could not feel which could supply more good food taste and health food quality to compare supermarkets specially. Otherwise, although, supermarkets could provide cheaper ready cooked meals to satisfy who to feel good food taste and health food quality. Due to ready meal manufacturers had new techniques to develop ready meals which preserve taste and texture, which still making them easy to use to eat by the consumers.

Furthermore, great advances in distribution management, in particular the use of information technology to control inventories, has allowed fresh , chilled ready meals to be effectively and efficiently distributed to supermarkets or restaurants without the need for freezing or added preservatives. Creating healthy food and eating environments view describes an ecological framework for conceptualizing the many food environments and conditions that influence food choices, with an emphasis on current knowledge was been regarding the home, child care, school, work site, retail store and restaurant settings. The status of measurement and evaluation of nutrition environment and the need of action to improve health are highlighted in marketing environment. More processed and convenience foods are available in large portion sizes and which were supplied at relatively low prices at supermarkets. Parents are working larger hours, there are fewer family meals and more meals are eaten away from home. The school food environment is remarkably different. It seemed that it would be changed in the marketing environment on sales of ready cooked meals to supermarket more easily. Due to supermarkets' cooked meals should focus on selling high calorie and low nutrition foods are available in multiple venues throughout the school student client group target because it was possible that supermarkets could sell ready cooked ready meals prices were more cheaper to compare to restaurants or school canters' cooked meals provided prices.

The effects of change in the marketing environment on sales of ready meals which indicated that consumers chose prefer to buy ready cooked meals from supermarkets. It seemed that a restaurant market failure could be caused to arise. For example, there was poor information on the part of food (ready cooked meals) to provide to the restaurant about the foods that consumers in a location(place) would demand for a given price to compare to the supermarket sale prices. The restaurant would lose clients if which cooked the kind of meals to sell higher price to compare to the supermarket sale of the kind of cooked ready meals price possibly. Large size supermarkets could sell cheaper ready cooked meals to low income group clients. It could cause competition to constitute a market failure to small size supermarkets. If the small size supermarkets lacked good information on the true food (ready cooked meals) with concentrations to sell cheaper prices, then this ready cooked meal market failure was one potential reason why small size supermarkets did not locate to close to the large supermarkets. Due to supermarkets grew in size would influence clients' choice to buy the numbers of cooked foods (ready meals) products. Moreover, The advent of computerized logistics and inventory systems were integrated with the large size supermarkets themselves occurred between the 1980 years and 1990 years .

So large size supermarkets were reliance on their own distribution and cooked food (ready meals) inventory systems along with larger supermarket sizes to allow super center to change to sell ready cooked meals at lower prices. Supermarkets marketing can promote healthful eating by increasing availability, affordability or restricting / de-marketing unhealthy foods to sell cooked Food (ready meals) marketing strategy at supermarkets, including labelling, packaging, pricing and point of sale advertising. Consumers' cost saving efforts and income and ready cooked meals prices increasing or decreasing factors can drive the choice of supermarkets as well as cooked meal products use of coupons and loyalty cards bargain shopping is another factor to influence their choice. Private label or store (supermarket) brands are taking an increasing share of consumers shopping dollars as the importance of brands. Supermarket shoppers stated priorities are cooked food (ready meals) quality or taste and price and healthy cooked food (ready meals) choices.

However, supermarket shoppers' buying behaviors don't always reflect on favor healthful foods. Due to demand for locally grown cooked food is increasing. Anyway, restaurant meals are changed to supermarket to sell, which decide what kinds of meals to stock and how many of different kinds of meals to stock and how much variety of kinds of meals to offer to any one supermarket as well as supermarket shoppers prefer fewer options, provided that their preferred brand or cooked food (ready meals) products are available. The designs of supermarket ready cooked meal products and packaging to supermarket to sell is the focus of unusual colors or shape which can be used to increase interest and is specially pervasive among fun foods to compare to restaurant meals. Package design, including where text and images are placed, which can influences cooked foods (supermarket ready meals repurchasing again).The influence of design differs by the type of display consumer segments seek (convenience, information or images) and ready cooked meals package sizes have a relatively strong influence on consumption; larger ready cooked meals packages might increase per-use consumption ,but smaller packages might not improve self regulation and might not actually increase total consumption.

In conclusion, I suggest that this ready meal manufacturers need to give more attention to be paid to food sellers, such as supermarkets' competitive differentiation and understanding the way in which customers attribute value to its ready meal products choice. Moreover, many consumers have become increasingly concerned about the health implication of the food they eat, so ready meal manufacturers will need to continue responding to such concerns. For example, who have responded with a range of low calorie meals, and addressed specific, sometimes transient, health fads, with respect to trans-fatty acids and omega 3 supplements of these cooked meal ingredients. Many consumers have also become concerned about the ecological environment and some supermarket suppliers, such as Marks and Spencer have incorporated sustainability agendas into their ready meals, for example by reducing packaging and sourcing supplies from sustainable sources. Thus, it caused ready meal manufacturers why who needed to give more attention to concern how supermarkets helped them to sell cooked ready meals in this foods market.

Critically discuss the link between the economic environment and sales of ready meals in supermarket. The macro environment, it describes things that are beyond the immediate environment but can nevertheless affect the organization. Such as the ready meal manufacturers in its macro environment, including the economic environment which can cause the manufacturers sell ready meal numbers whether which can sell more or less to different exported countries due to the exported countries' unemployment ratios, GDP and Government policies etc factors influence. Economic theory can help to explain why it can influence consumer behavior. In food sale market, it can include consumer behavior and demand side as well as retailer behavior and supply side two issues.

Consumer behavior and demand side issue, such as the exported countries' consumer whose knowledge of the nutritional benefits of foods whether which prices were raised to choose to buy reasonably as well as retailer behavior and supply side issues, such as investing for developing a restaurant or supermarket in an underserved area whether the types of meals choices which are valued or which are not valued to buy to offer to clients from imports. On the other hand, economic environment factor, individual income can influence who chooses the type, quantity and quality of food that is purchased for a house holder and it also influenced the cooking and storage facilities available in a household to influence food choice.

On the other way, economic environment variation factor can also influence food access across areas. It is important to understand the economic conditions that may contribute to food deserts, that is the costs that food retail businesses face and the choice available to consumers who want to buy foods. Economic environment factor considers the consumer and demand factors, business and supply factors and the market conditions that interact to create differences in the food retail environment across areas and subpopulations. In general, high income meal client group can accept to choose to go to supermarkets or restaurants to spend than low income meal client group. The impact of the economic environment on sales of ready meals is such as an individual get richer, who can afford to buy ready prepared foods, rather than spend time and effort to prepare to cook them at home. It seemed that low income consumers were decreasing to eat meals at expensive restaurant to the alternative of relatively cheap ready prepared meals at home. Research could also consider how consumer knowledge and preferences and the time cost tradeoffs affect consumer decisions of which foods to eat and whether to make or to buy prepared foods from supermarkets or to eat at restaurant meals . Travel costs and time costs of acquiring foods as well as the time costs of preparing foods (meals) are also likely to affect demand for particular foods. Research on price variation at the local level and demand models could also be used to help determine which factors contribute to differences in access to food retailers. Price is also major determinant of food (meal) demand.

The higher, the price of a food(meal), the lower the meal quantity demanded. On the other hand, the higher the price of a substitute food (meal), the higher demand will be for that food (meal) item. Given the budget constraints of low income consumers and the price of some specific foods (meals), low income consumers may substitute higher priced foods (meals) with lower priced foods(e.g. hamburger for steak or canned fruits for fresh fruits). Considering restaurants foods purchasing choice, such as economies of scale, which is when the costs of operating a restaurant decreases as restaurant size increases and economies of scope, which is when the costs decrease as more meals variety increases, suggests that larger restaurants that offer greater variety can offer lower meal prices. Both factors may account for the ability of larger restaurants to survive more easily than smaller restaurants. Considering supermarkets foods purchasing choice, it is possible that food retailers (supermarkets) actually have some market power, especially in setting where there are few competitors to close. It would have an incentive to increase food (ready meal) price and restrict foods(ready meals) supply quantities to increase profit. Supply side conditions, such as economies of scale, it could lead to (ready meal) food retailers (supermarkets) to have more market power, if it was not close between supermarkets. Individual behavior to make healthy choices can occur only in a supportive economic environment with accessible and affordable healthy food choices. Hence, food environment and sale strategies is needed to consider to adopt the exported countries' economic change.

Food marketing client target groups can include home parents, students and working people groups mainly and marketing and economic environment factors would cause food choices and these factors impact health and nutrition and the focus on the connections between people and their environments.

In conclusion, macro level economic environmental factors play a more indirect role but have a substantial and powerful effect on what people eat. Macro level factors operate within the larger society, include food marketing, social norms, food production and distribution systems, agriculture policies and economic price structures as well as social environmental to influence within the home, such as model of healthful dietary intake by parents feeding style, frequent family meals may promote healthful food consumption among children.

www.ingramcontent.com/pod-product-compliance
Ingram Content Group UK Ltd.
Pitfield, Milton Keynes, MK11 3LW, UK
UKHW022017190726
13853UKWH00005B/1985

9 798888 699386